Cooking with Beer

Cookbook Resources, LLC
Highland Village, Texas

Cooking with Beer

1st Printing - March 2010

International Standard Book Number: 978-1-59769-006-5

Library of Congress Control Number: 2009039924

Library of Congress Cataloging-in-Publication Data:

    Cooking with beer.
       p. cm.
    Includes index.
    ISBN 978-1-59769-006-5
    1. Cookery (Beer) 2. Beer. 3. Cookery. 4. Beer. I. Cookbook Resources, LLC. II. Title.

    TX726.3.C63 2009
    641.6'23--dc22

                            2009039924

Cover illustration by Matthew Holmes

Edited, Designed, Published and Manufactured in the United States of America by
Cookbook Resources, LLC
541 Doubletree Drive
Highland Village, Texas 75077

Toll free 866-229-2665

www.cookbookresources.com

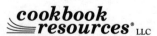

Bringing Family and Friends to the Table

Move Over Wine. Hello Beer!

Wine, long flaunted for its sophisticated flavors and beneficial effects, has a new rival as beer becomes more prominent in today's food experiences.

Cooking with beer and the pairing of beer and food are well in gear and hitting worldwide markets.

Belgium, as the world capital of beer, produces more than 800 varieties of beer. And production all over the world has grown significantly not only in quantity, but also in variety and quality.

This cookbook is a basic starter kit for cooking with beer. It's not the definitive guide to cooking with beer by any stretch, but it is a friendly, easy-to-understand, get-the-big-picture type book that is a great first read and first step to cooking with beer.

It has an easy glossary that explains the most important terms while leaving the more obscure words, phrases and processes to more sophisticated sources. Most recipes are simple enough not to intimidate the novice cook, but not so simple as to bore the advanced cook. The recipes are good ones to start with, to find a few favorites and to live with for years to come.

The cookbook is also filled with interesting history and facts scattered throughout its pages that provide an entertaining element to recipe searches.

The cookbook takes what is sure to be a very sophisticated subject and makes it simple from the very beginning. It doesn't get so bogged down in culinary rules and gastronomical nuances that the fun is lost.

We're explaining a new way to approach beer and food by pairing flavors, but when it's all said and done, if you like it, it's good.

Contents

Contents

> *More and more statistical studies are finding that family meals play
> a significant role in childhood development. Children who eat with their
> families four or more nights per week are healthier, make better grades, score
> higher on aptitude tests and are less likely to have problems with drugs.*

Dedication

With a mission of helping you bring family and friends to the table, Cookbook Resources strives to make family meals and entertaining friends simple, easy and delicious.

We recognize the importance of sharing meals together as a means of building family bonds with memories and traditions that will be treasured for a lifetime. It is an opportunity to sit down with each other and share more than food.

This cookbook is dedicated with gratitude and respect for all those who show their love with homecooked meals and bring family and friends to the table.

(Even though this cookbook uses beer in the recipes, the alcoholic content is reduced by cooking and the flavors remain.)

Look for these icons in the cookbook.

 Fun Facts or Tips About Beer

Entertaining Quotes About Beer

 Slow Cooker Recipes

Microwave Recipes

What Makes Beer, Beer?

Short Answer: Beer is a generic term that means an alcoholic beverage using fermented, malted grains. There are two types or categories of beer: ales and lagers.

Long Answer: Beer is made from grains, yeast, water and hops. Barley is the most traditional grain. Grains are soaked in water until they begin to germinate or malt. They are then roasted which releases starches that become fermented sugars. Yeast is added and creates alcohol and carbon dioxide.

Malts have a sweet flavor and hops have a bitter taste. Hops are added to balance the sweetness of the malts. Top-fermenting yeasts make ales. Bottom-fermenting yeasts make lagers. The variables of grains, yeast, water, hops, temperatures, roasting, time stored, alcohol content, viscosity and color produce hundreds of varieties of ales and lagers, all of which are beers.

Types of Ale

Ales are alcoholic beverages brewed with barley and fermented at high temperatures with top-fermenting yeasts. These may be pale or very dark in color. Ales usually have a fruity taste.

Bitters   Bitters are usually draft (draught) beers similar to pale ales and not regularly bottled but served in pubs.

Brown Ales   Brown ales are usually a reddish-brown color and have sweet, chocolate and fruity flavors. They are considered thirst-quenchers in England. In the U.S. they have a higher alcohol content, but still have the same flavors.

Continued next page...

Continued from previous page...

India Pale Ales   India pale ale, referred to as IPA, has a stronger flavor than pale ale. It is brewed with hops added after fermentation which produces the hoppier, stronger flavor.

Pale Ales   Pale ales are lighter in color than the darker stouts and porters. Malts are roasted for less time, giving a slightly honey, caramel flavor.

Porters   Porter has a dark color with a roasted flavor. It usually has more alcohol content than regular ales or lagers, but is not as full-bodied as stouts. Porters and stouts are similar, but porters are lighter in color and body.

Stouts   Stouts are very dark and brewed with roasted malt or barley with top-fermenting yeast giving it a very robust flavor. It is a generic term used to describe the strongest or stoutest beers.

Types of Lager

Lagers are alcoholic beverages brewed at low temperatures with bottom-fermenting yeast and are stored in cool temperatures to settle imperfections and produce a crisp taste. These are usually clear, light-colored beers, but some may be darker.

Bocks   Bock beers are usually dark in color and served in the fall and winter. They are strong with a sweet taste that overshadows the presence of a hop bitterness. Bock is a German word meaning strong.

Dopplebocks   Dopplebock means double bock, has a high alcohol content and is usually a dark tan or dark brown color.

Continued next page...

Continued from previous page...

Hefeweizens   *Hefe* is the German word for "yeast" and *weizen* is the German word for "wheat". It usually has a light, refreshing taste.

Lambics   Lambic is a pilsner-style beer made only in Belgium. It is brewed by fermenting malted barley and unmalted wheat.

Light Beers   Light beer is an American pilsner-style beer brewed with a lower alcohol content and fewer calories.

Pilsners   Pilsner is a pale lager first brewed in what is today the Czech Republic using a bottom-fermenting yeast. Most American beers are pilsner-style.

Weizens   *Weizen* is a German word meaning "wheat" and is used to describe beer made with malted wheat.

Draught (Draft) Beers

Draught (or draft) beers are any of the above beers served from a tap that runs from a keg or barrel.

Beer, if drunk in moderation, softens the temper, cheers the spirit and promotes health.
—Thomas Jefferson

Beer Talk

If you're going to cook with beer, you need to know a few basic terms so you can navigate the growing number of beers on the market. We'll start at the beginning to get you started and getting started is the most important thing.

Ales . . . . one of the two categories of beer; made with top-fermenting yeast and brewed at warm temperature; most popular in the U.K., Germany, Belgium, Ireland and Canada; sweet, full-bodied, fruity taste; hops give slightly bitter taste to balance sweetness; fruity flavors may be described as apple, banana, pear, prune and pineapple

Barley . . . . cereal grain used in the brewing of beer

Beer . . . . a generic term used to describe alcoholic beverages made from fermenting malted grains. There are two categories of beer: ale and lager.

Bitter . . . . description of taste from hops added to beer for flavor; felt on back of tongue

Brew pub . . . . establishment that brews and sells at least 50% of its own beer on the premises

Caramel . . . . cooked sugar used to add color and alcohol to beer; a low-priced substitute for more expensive malted barley

Caramel malt . . . gives beer its color and flavor; has high concentration of unfermentable sugars that sweeten the flavor and help with head retention

Continued next page...

Continued from previous page...

Clovelike. . . . . some wheat beers have a spicy flavor similar to cloves as a result of the use of a wild yeast

Craft beer. . . . . . . brewed in a small, independent, traditional brewery that produces less than 2,000,000 barrels annually; these breweries are sometimes called microbreweries or brew pubs

Cream ale. . . . . . . golden, slightly sweet, light-bodied ale; smooth taste

Draft beer . . . . (also spelled draught) any beer dispensed from a tap connected to a keg or barrel

Ester . . . . naturally created compound that produces flavors of flowers and fruits

Fermentation . . . . process by which sugars are converted into ethyl alcohol and carbon dioxide through the action of yeast

Fruity (Estery). . . . flavors of banana, apples, pears or other fruits produced by certain types of yeast fermented at high temperatures

Head retention . . . helps beer hold in carbonation and flavor for its peak taste after it is poured into a glass

Hefe. . . . . German word meaning "yeast"; used mostly with wheat (weizen) beers to state that the beer was bottled with the yeast in suspension (hefe weizen); these beers are usually frothy, may be cloudy and are very refreshing

Continued next page...

Continued from previous page...

Hoppy . . . . refers to aroma and not bitterness although hops and bitterness are related

Hops . . . . flower cone of climbing perennial that is used to stabilize the aroma and to balance the flavor with its bitterness added to sweetness of malts; also adds antibiotic favorable to the activity of yeasts used in brewing

Lagers . . . . one of the two categories of beer; made with bottom-fermenting yeast and brewed at cool temperatures; most popular in the U.S.; light in color and mild flavor; pilsner-style beer; best known brands in the U.S. are Budweiser, Busch, Coors and Michelob; is a more crisp-tasting beer than ales

Light beer . . . . brewed in similar way as ales and lagers, but with less alcohol and fewer calories; found mostly in the U.S.

Malt . . . . basic ingredient of beer created when barley is changed from insoluble starch to soluble substances and sugar

Malt liquor . . . term used in the U.S. to describe a fermented beverage with 7% to 8% alcohol content

Mouthfeel . . . term used to describe a thin or full consistency of beer

Pale ale . . . . . . hearty, robust, flavored ale; color ranges from golden to dark amber; lightly carbonated; very good paired with spicy foods; India pale ale is one of the most famous

Continued next page...

Continued from previous page...

Pasteurization. . . heating of beer to stabilize it microbiologically

Porters . . . . characterized by darkness in color with rich, roasted malt, slightly bitter flavor; known for creamy head

Salty . . . . flavor of table salt; felt on the side of the tongue

Shelf life . . . . amount of time a beer will retain its peak drinkability; commercially produced beers have a shelf-life of about four months

Stouts . . . . very similar to porters which are characterized by darkness in color with rich, roasted malt; slightly bitter flavor; known for creamy head; stout is more heavily hopped and bitter than porter

Sweet. . . . . flavor of sugar; felt on the front of the tongue

Tart . . . . taste caused by acidic flavors

Yeast . . . . microorganism in fungus family

You can't be a real country unless you have a beer and an airline — it helps if you have some kind of a football team, or some nuclear weapons, but at the very least you need a beer.

–Frank Zappa

Cooking with Beer

Here are some broad generalizations to help you start cooking with beer. As you progress with your culinary prowess, you can research more sophisticated pairings. Decisions about beer and food can get as complex as wine and food.

Generalizations:

- Light, refreshing beers go well with light foods.

- Full-flavored beers go well with full-flavored, hearty foods.

- The flavors of beers will be intensified in the cooking process.

- The best beers should be used with the best foods for the best results.

- Use beers you are familiar with and like and use them in moderation.

- Don't boil beer. It brings out the bitterness of the hops.

- Use a little beer instead of wine or broths.

Continued next page...

Continued from previous page...

Cooking Methods:

Baking   Beer adds moisture and leavening. The carbonation is a leavening agent and lightens the finished product.

Braising   Beer is a very good liquid to use with foods that are cooked in liquid on low temperatures for a long time in the oven or on a closed grill.

Frying   Beer batters used in frying foods will create a lighter, fluffier batter for a lighter, crispier crust.

Deglazing   A little beer is very good to use to scrape off brown pieces of foods that remain in the skillet after sauteing.

Marinating   Beer is a great marinade because it adds flavor and breaks down the protein to tenderize meats. Beer can also be used with fruit to add flavor.

Poaching   A little beer with fish is a nice addition of flavor, especially a wheat or fruit beer.

Simmering   Beer is great when simmered, but never boil beer because the bitterness of the hops will come through strongly.

Spritz   Spray a little beer on meat on the grill to add a little moisture on the outside.

Pairing Food and Beer

The purpose of using beer in cooking is to add flavor and moisture to the outside and inside of foods. It is important to use complementary flavors, not too much of any one ingredient, and don't overcook it. The following pairings are not hard-and-fast but will at least give you a starting point. The fun part about cooking with beer is experimenting.

Strong-flavored beers such as stouts and porters should be paired with strong-flavored, heavy foods.

Light-flavored beers such as most lagers, pilsners, wheat beers, hefeweizens and sweetened ales should be paired with light-flavored foods.

Mild, medium-range flavors of beer such as amber ales, brown ales and pale ales should be paired with mid-range flavors of food.

Food	Type of Beer
Beef, lamb, game	Porter, brown ale, fruity pale ale, amber ale
Bacon burger	Pale ale, cream ale
Hamburgers	Amber ale, cream ale, pale ale
Breads	
Waffles, pancakes	Pale lager
Cajun foods	India pale ale, stout, porter, bock

Continued next page...

Continued from previous page...

Food	Type of Beer
Cheeses	
Aged cheddar	Stout, porter
Mild cheddar	Pale ale, brown ale
Feta and goat	Belgian witbier
Smoked gouda	Belgian witbier, amber lager
Chevre	American wheat ale, pilsner
Aged gouda	Hefeweizen, stout
Brie	Blonde ale, cream ale, American lager
Blue	Pale ale
Provolone	India pale ale
Gruyere	Amber ale
Gorgonzola	Porter
White cheddar	Bock
Chicken	Ales
Chicken wings, hot	India pale ale, stout, porter
Chicken wings, mild	Lager, pilsner
Chocolate	Stout (chocolate, oatmeal, raspberry), porter
Dark chocolate	Imperial, lambic
Sweet	Barley wine
Creamy Soups	Pilsner
Desserts	Dark ale, cream stout
Pecan pie	Brown ale
Espresso and coffee-flavored desserts	Porter
Caramel	Barley wine
Fried Foods	Pilsner, pale ale
Jalapeno poppers	India pale ale, stout, dark ale
Fruit and fruit desserts	Fruit beer, wheat beer, pilsner
Berries	Hefeweizen
Citrus	Hefeweizen, Belgian witbier
Marinades	
Marinades for beef and pork	Brown ale, stout, porter
Marinades for fish and chicken	Pale ale
Mexican food	Mexican gold, amber lager

Continued next page...

Continued from previous page...

Food	Type of Beer
Nuts	
Dry roasted nuts	Pale ale, India pale ale, stout, porter
Peanuts	Nut brown ale, honey ale
Pasta	Amber ale
With red sauce	Amber ale, cream ale, pale ale
With vegetables and herbs	Blonde ale, Hefeweizen
Pizza	Domestic lager, brown ale, amber ale
Pork	Stout, Vienna-style lager, German wheat, Marzen
Barbecue	Amber ale, bock, porter
Sausage, bratwurst	Bock, brown ale, German dark lager
Ribs	Amber ale, cream ale, pale ale
Weisswurst (white sausage)	Hefeweizen
Roasted pork	Brown ale
Bacon	Porter
Salads	Pilsner, brown ale
Sandwiches	Amber ale
Sauces	
Rich or creamy	Stout, porter
Light	Hefeweizen
Peanut	Brown ale
Brown, savory	Stout
Sun-dried tomato reduction	Amber lager
Seafood	
Fish	Wheat beer, dry lager, dry pilsner
High-fat, oily fish (salmon, tuna)	Pilsner
Shellfish	Pilsner, stout, wheat, Hefeweizen
Shellfish with butter	Pilsner, light lager
Shellfish with red sauce	Pale ale, amber ale
Sushi	Japanese lager
Ceviche	Belgian witbier
Oysters on half shell	Stout
Spicy foods	Blonde ale, American wheat ale
Stews and hearty soups	Brown ale, porter
Thai foods	India pale ale, stout, porter

How to Get the Most Out of Drinking Beer

Temperature

■ Serve beer at optimal temperatures to get the full flavors of the beer.

■ As a general rule, lagers, pilsners and light-tasting beers that are thirst-quenching and easy to drink should be colder than robust ales, stouts and porters.

Type of Beer	Temperature Range
Fruit Beers	40° to 50° (5° to 10° C)
Wheat beers and pale lagers	45° to 50° (7° to 10° C)
Pale ales and dark lagers	50° to 55° (10° to 13° C)
Strong ales and Belgian ales	50° to 55° (10° to 13° C)
Dark ales, stouts and porters	55° to 60° (13° to 15° C)

How to Pour Beer

■ When pouring beer into a glass, hold the glass almost horizontally and pour beer down the side of the glass. This holds in the flavor and carbonation.

■ When the bottle is about half full, begin to turn the glass vertically and pour beer into the middle of the glass. The foam is very important to hold the flavors.

Continued next page...

Continued from previous page...

■ Stop pouring with just enough room at the top of the glass for the foam to go to the top, but not spill over.

Beer Glasses and Their Care

■ Don't wash beer glasses in the dishwasher.

■ Soap residue stays on the glasses and has an effect on the flavors of the beer.

■ The best way to clean beer glasses is to rinse them thoroughly and let them air dry.

■ Only use beer glasses for beer.

■ Residue from other beverages will remain on glasses even though they've been washed.

■ A trend in beer-drinking circles is to use particular glasses with particular varieties of beer.

■ When you determine your favorite beers, you may enjoy researching beer glasses to see if they add to your pleasure.

Enjoy the Experience

■ When drinking beer, think about the flavors of each variety and how they might pair with food.

■ This is the first step to cooking with beer and injecting new flavors into your food experience.

The fastest method to chill beer is to put cold water, then ice (be sure it's heavy with ice) and salt in a cooler or galvanized tub (or a bathtub). Salt lowers the freezing point of water (just like in an ice cream freezer) and beer cools quickly.

How to Get Started Taste-Testing Beer

The following is a list of well-known, popular styles of beer with some name brands associated with each style. This will at least give you a starting point from which to explore more styles and more brands.

Choose the flavors you like and pair them with food. Beer does not add its own flavors, but enhances existing flavors of food.

Type of Beer	Description	Brand Names
American Light Lager	This is a pilsner-style beer, light in color, very effervescent, slightly sweet, lightly hopped and not always brewed with barley malt.	American: *Budweiser, Miller, Coors*
Pilsner	Pilsner was the world's first pale ale. It was originally brewed in Pilsen in Bohemia (today part of the Czech Republic) as a full-bodied, bottom-fermented pale ale.	German: *Beck's, Bitburger Premier, Konig Pilsner* Belgian: *Stella Artois*
Pale Ale or British Bitter	This pale ale varies by flavors and alcoholic content. It is called ESP (Extra Special Bitter) in the U.S. meaning a pale ale with less alcohol.	British: *Greene King IPA, Flowers IPA*
India Pale Ale	Pale ale that is more hopped than regular pale ale. It was created to withstand long voyages between the U.K. and its protectorates.	American: *Liberty Ale*
Brown Ale	Brown ale is a traditional British, top-fermented ale that is a little sweeter and darker than pale ale.	British: *Mann's Original Brown Ale, Newcastle Brown Ale*

Continued next page...

Continued from previous page...

Type of Beer	Description	Brand Names
Strong Ale	Strong ale has a high alcohol content, is very dark and has a very sweet flavor. Scottish ale has a high alcohol content with a hint of caramel and a slightly smoky flavor. Bock beer is also a strong ale and has the highest alcohol content, as much as 10%. It is brewed with a top-fermenting yeast and is aged for at least a month.	Scottish: *McEwan's Scottish Ale* German: *Steinbach Bock, Schell Bock*
Porter	Porter is similar to strong ale, but is darker than amber and lighter than stout.	American: *Pottsville Porter*
Stout	Stout is a very dark, roasted malt beer that is full-flavored and a tradition in Ireland.	Irish: *Guinness Stout*
Wheat Beer	Wheat beer uses wheat grain with dark and light malted wheat and caramelized malt. It is usually aged several weeks in cold storage.	Belgian: *Paulaner Hefeweizen*
Belgian Beers	Belgium is considered the beer capital of the world.	
	Flanders red ale is the best example of red beers brewed in Belgium and uses two different hops and five kinds of yeast.	Belgian: *Rodenbach*
	Lambic beer is a top-fermented, red, cherry-flavored brew with a sparkling taste and is best served in a champagne glass.	Belgian: *Lindeman's Kriek*
	Belgian strong is the quintessential pale strong ale. It is brewed with Danish barley malt and undergoes three fermentations.	Belgian: *Duvel*

Snacks
&
Drinks

Oktoberfest

The largest festival in the world is Oktoberfest held annually in Munich, Bavaria, Germany to celebrate "liquid gold". In Munich, more than 6,000,000 people come together to celebrate the world's greatest beers. Today people celebrate Oktoberfest all over the world.

Oktoberfest

O ktoberfest is a 16-day celebration with beer in the starring role. It is celebrated all over the world, but the world's largest festival welcomes more than 6,000,000 people to Munich's Oktoberfest grounds to drink German beer and eat German food.

Oktoberfest grew out of the celebration of the marriage of Crown Prince Ludwig of Bavaria and Princess Therese of Saxe-Hildburghausen on October 12, 1810. Since that time the tradition has been carried on not only in Germany, but around the world.

Beer has been considered a food, a staple in every kitchen and a necessity of life throughout history. It became especially important to all people when it was clear that longer life spans for the wealthy were the results of the wealthy drinking beer instead of water.

Peasants drank unfiltered, contaminated water which spread disease and death. When peasants began drinking more beer and less water, the life expectancy grew to equal that of the wealthy.

The role of beer throughout history is quite evident and can be traced back as far as 8,000 years ago. The fact that Munich's Oktoberfest is the largest celebration in the world is not only fitting, but in keeping with the major role beer has played in society's evolution.

Among the oldest laws concerning the regulation of food or drink were the Bavarian Purity Laws passed in 1516. They stated that Bavarian beer should only be made of water, hops and barley. Standardizing Bavaria's beer process became the first real step to brewing excellence.

Continued next page...

Continued from previous page...

Puritan colonists in the New World originally planned to have the first celebration feast in Virginia, but the *Mayflower's* sailors forced the landing at Plymouth Rock. The beer supply was running low and the sailors wanted enough beer for the return voyage.

Traditional German foods associated with Oktoberfest include dishes from the list below. Several of these dishes use beer as one of the ingredients and may be found in this cookbook.

Hendl	roasted chicken
Wurstel	sausage
Brezel	pretzel
Schweinsbraten	roast pork
Steckerlfisch	fish on a stick
Knodeln	potato dumplings

Look for these recipes to help create your own special Oktoberfest.

Easy Breezy Brie

¼ cup (½ stick) butter	55 g
½ cup minced onions	40 g
1 clove garlic, minced	
12 – 14 large button mushrooms, chopped	
¼ cup Samuel Adams Boston ale	60 ml
½ cup finely chopped pecans or	
walnuts, toasted	55 g/65 g
2 small brie rounds	

■ Preheat oven to 350° (175° C).

■ Melt butter in skillet and add onions, garlic and mushrooms. Cook until onions and garlic are transparent.

■ Add beer and cook slowly over medium-high heat until beer evaporates. Heat brie rounds in oven for 5 minutes or until center is soft.

■ Spread onions mixture over brie rounds and serve immediately. Serves about 6 to 8.

> *As a general rule, the shelf life of commercially brewed beer, stored properly, is about four months at the most. During this time beer is at its best flavor.*

Fancy Easy Breezy Brie

Ingredients for Easy Breezy Brie (see page 26)
1 (4 sheet) package frozen puff pastry dough, thawed
Parchment paper
1 egg white, lightly beaten

■ Preheat oven to 350° (175° C).

■ Make topping for Easy Breezy Brie (see directions in previous recipe). Chill brie well and slice the 2 rounds in half horizontally.

■ Place each slice of brie in center of 1 pastry dough sheet. Place one-forth of topping on brie slice, cheese side up, and bring pastry sides of sheet up to center.

■ Twist slightly to seal pastry dough covering brie. Repeat process with remaining brie.

■ Line baking sheet with parchment paper and place pastries on top of paper. Brush pastries with egg white. Bake for about 3 to 5 minutes or until pastry browns slightly. Serves about 12 for appetizers.

A woman drove me to drink and I didn't even have the decency to thank her.
—W.C. Fields

Good-Time Cheese Chaser

This is very easy to make and fun at parties.

1 (8 ounce) package shredded cheddar cheese	225 g
1 (8 ounce) package shredded Swiss cheese	225 g
1 (8 ounce) package shredded mozzarella cheese	225 g
2 teaspoons mayonnaise	10 ml
2 teaspoons Worcestershire sauce	10 ml
1 teaspoon dry mustard	5 ml
½ teaspoon minced garlic	2ml
½ cup beer	125 ml
Crackers or celery	

■ Mix cheeses in large bowl with mayonnaise, Worcestershire sauce, dry mustard, garlic and enough beer to make mixture into spreading consistency.

■ Pack into 3-cup (750 ml) mold and refrigerate. Remove from mold and serve at room temperature. Serve with crackers or celery. Yields about 3 cups (750 ml).

For the best tasting beer, don't use a frosted mug or glass. As the beer hits the glass, the ice melts, dilutes the beer and changes the serving temperature.

Beer Cheese

1 (16 ounce) package shredded sharp cheddar cheese	455 g
1 tablespoon Worcestershire sauce	15 ml
½ cup beer	125 ml
½ teaspoon dry mustard	2 ml
½ teaspoon hot pepper sauce	2 ml
2 cloves garlic, minced	
2 teaspoons minced onion	2 ml

■ Mix all ingredients in blender or with electric mixer. Pack into bowl or crock and cover tightly.

■ This may be stored in refrigerator for up to 2 weeks. Yields about 4 cups (1 L).

If you ever reach total enlightenment while drinking beer, I bet it makes beer shoot out your nose.
—Jack Handy

Oktoberfest Fondue

Fondue:

1 (12 ounce) package shredded sharp cheddar cheese	340 g
1 (8 ounce) package shredded gruyere	225 g
1 rounded tablespoon flour	15 ml
1 cup German lager beer, room temperature	250 ml
2 tablespoons spicy brown mustard	30 g
Hot sauce	

■ Mix cheeses with flour in medium saucepan. Heat over medium-low heat and pour in beer a little at a time. Stir constantly while cooking and be sure not to boil beer or cheese.

■ Add mustard and a little hot sauce to taste. It works best to use a wooden spoon and thoroughly mix cheese and other ingredients. Pour into warm fondue pot and serve hot. Yields 3 cups (750 ml).

Items for dunking:

1½ pounds cooked, browned knockwurst or bratwurst	680 g
Cauliflower florets	
Pumpernickel or sourdough bread, cubed	
Gherkin pickles	

■ Spear with fondue forks and dunk in fondue.

Cheesy Beer Fondue

¼ cup (½ stick) butter	55 g
¼ cup flour	30 g
1 (12 ounce) bottle lager	355 ml
½ teaspoon Worcestershire sauce	2 ml
¼ teaspoon dry mustard	1 ml
¼ teaspoon cayenne pepper	1 ml
1 (16 ounce) package shredded cheddar cheese	455 g
Day-old bread, cubed	

■ Melt butter in medium saucepan over medium heat. Whisk in flour and cook for 1 to 2 minutes while stirring constantly to make roux.

■ Add beer and cook on medium-high, but do not boil. Reduce heat, simmer and stir occasionally until mixture thickens to the consistency of whipping cream.

■ Add Worcestershire, mustard and cayenne and stir thoroughly. Add cheese, one-fourth at a time, and melt cheese after each addition.

■ Stir fondue until it is smooth. Turn into fondue pot and serve with cubed day-old bread. Serves 4.

 Did you know that beer has been brewed for more than 8,000 years and was considered a staple in every household?

Easy Beer and Cheese Dip

1 large onion, finely chopped	
2 tablespoons butter	30 g
1 cup beer	250 ml
1 (32 ounce) box Mexican Velveeta® cheese	910 g
Tortilla chips	

- ■ Cook onion in butter in large saucepan, but do not brown; add beer.

- ■ Cut cheese into large chunks and add to onion-beer mixture and cook on medium-low heat, stirring constantly until all cheese melts.

- ■ Serve with tortilla chips. Yields 1 quart (1 L).

I am a firm believer in the people. If given the truth, they can be depended upon to meet any national crisis. The great point is to bring them the real facts, and beer.

—Abraham Lincoln

Beer Con Queso Dip

1 (16 ounce) package shredded Mexican
    Velveeta® cheese   455 g
1 (8 ounce) package shredded cheddar cheese 225 g
2 tablespoons flour   15 g
1 small onion, minced
1 tablespoon butter   15 ml
1 (12 ounce) can beer   355 ml
½ cup chopped tomatoes   90 g
¼ - ½ cup chopped jalapeno slices,
    seeds removed*   25 - 45 g
Tortilla chips

■ Toss cheeses with flour. Cook onion in heavy saucepan
with butter over low heat and stir until onion is
transparent.

■ Add beer, tomatoes and jalapenos and simmer for
5 minutes; do not boil. Add cheese-flour mixture,
½ cup (125 ml) at a time, to beer mixture and stir after
each addition until cheeses melts. Serve dip with chips.
Yields 5 cups (1.2 L).

TIP: Wear rubber gloves when handling jalapenos.

 Fermentation is the process that turns sugar into alcohol and carbon dioxide as a result of yeast.

Tipsy Chile Con Queso

2 (16 ounce) packages cubed Velveeta® cheese	2 (455 g)
1 (7 ounce) can diced green chilies	200 g
1 medium onion, chopped	
1 (12 ounce) can beer, divided	355 ml
1 (4 ounce) can taco sauce	115 g

- ■ In double boiler, melt cheese and stir constantly so cheese will not burn.

- ■ Add green chilies, onion, ¼ cup (60 ml) beer and taco sauce and mix well. Thin cheese sauce with a little more beer, if needed, and drink the rest. Serve warm with chips. Yields 3 cups (750 ml).

Beer can be used as a glaze or in a sauce for chicken and beef. The flavors added are similar to the flavors one tastes at the back of the tongue when drinking a beer. As a general rule of thumb, the more bitter or heartier the flavor, the heartier the meal should be.

Rama-Dama Amber Dunk

1 (16 ounce) package shredded extra-sharp cheddar cheese	455 g
½ cup amber beer	125 ml
3 - 5 cloves garlic, minced	
¼ - 1 teaspoon hot pepper sauce	1 - 5 ml
Chips, crackers and/or pretzels	

- ■ Place cheese in blender and slowly pour in beer while processing. Blend with garlic and hot sauce. Taste several times to check seasonings.

- ■ Refrigerate and serve with chips or crackers. It's also great with pretzels. Yields 2 cups (500 ml).

An intelligent man is sometimes forced to be drunk to spend time with fools.
—For Whom the Bell Tolls, Ernest Hemingway

Cheesy Beer-Spinach Dip

1 (12 ounce) can beer	355 ml
1 (16 ounce) package shredded colby Jack cheese	455 g
3 tablespoons flour	25 g
1 (16 ounce) frozen chopped spinach, thawed, well drained*	455 g
½ teaspoon garlic salt	2 ml
½ teaspoon dried basil	2 ml

■ Bring beer almost to boiling in medium saucepan over medium heat. Lower heat; slowly stir in cheese and flour.

■ Cook and stir until cheese melts, but does not boil or get to bubbly stage. Mix spinach, garlic salt and basil into beer mixture. Serve warm. Yields 4 cups (1 L).

TIP: Squeeze spinach between paper towels to remove excess moisture completely.

The word "hefe" is German for "yeast" and is used to describe beers that are bottled or kegged with the yeast in suspension. Wheat (weizen) beer is an example of hefeweizen beer.

Guinness
Broccoli-Cheddar Dip

¼ cup minced onion	40 g
4 garlic cloves, minced	
2 tablespoons olive oil	30 ml
1 teaspoon dijon-style mustard	5 ml
1 (15 ounce) can Guinness® Draught beer	445 ml
1 (8 ounce) carton whipping cream, divided	250 ml
1 (16 ounce) package broccoli slaw	455 g
1 (16 ounce) package shredded cheddar cheese	455 g
Chips, crackers, pretzels, etc.	

- Saute onions and garlic in saucepan with oil until transparent. Add mustard and mix.

- Pour beer and ¾ cup (175 ml) cream in saucepan and cook on medium-low heat until mixture reduces by about half.

- Reduce heat to low and stir in most of cheddar cheese until it begins to melt. Add remaining cream, broccoli slaw and remaining cheese; slowly melt all cheese and mix all ingredients.

- Serve warm with chips, crackers, pretzels, etc. Yields 5½ cups (1.3 L).

Zippy Beer Dip

2 (8 ounce) packages cream cheese, softened   2 (225 g)
½ cup beer   125 ml
1 (1 ounce) packet ranch salad dressing mix   30 g
1 (8 ounce) package shredded Mexican
     4-cheese blend   225 g
1 (11 ounce) can Mexicorn®, drained   310 g
Chips

- Beat cream cheese, beer and ranch dressing with electric mixer. Stir in shredded cheese and Mexicorn®. Refrigerate 4 hours or overnight and serve with chips. Serves 4.

Clear Beer Dip

1 (8 ounce) package cream cheese   225 g
¼ cup beer   60 ml
1½ teaspoons paprika   7 ml
2 - 3 tablespoons hot pepper sauce   30 - 45 ml

- Melt cream cheese in heavy saucepan over medium-low heat. Stir in beer and seasonings and mix. Serve warm or cold. Yields 1 cup (250 ml).

Deadliest Catch Dip

1 (16 ounce) package cream cheese, softened	455 g
½ cup light beer	125 ml
1 (12 ounce) can crabmeat or 1 pound	
lump crabmeat, picked, drained	340 g/455 g
2 green onions with tops, minced	
2 tablespoons chopped celery	15 g
¼ teaspoon garlic powder	1 ml
1 teaspoon lemon juice	5 ml
1 teaspoon seasoned salt	5 ml
¼ - ½ teaspoon cayenne pepper	1 - 2 ml

■ Beat softened cream cheese with beer using electric mixer.

■ Add crabmeat, onions, celery, garlic powder, lemon juice and cayenne pepper and mix.

■ Refrigerate and serve. Serves 8 to 10.

A quart of ale is a dish for a king.
—William Shakespeare

Hot Clam Dip

1 (20 ounce) loaf round French bread	565 g
2 (8 ounce) packages cream cheese, softened	2 (225 g)
¼ cup mayonnaise	55 g
2 tablespoons beer	30 ml
2 teaspoons lime juice	10 ml
½ teaspoon hot pepper sauce	2 ml
1 teaspoon garlic salt	5 ml
3 (6.5 ounce) cans minced clams, drained	3 (185 g)

■ Preheat oven to 250° (120° C).

■ Cut off top of bread and set aside. Hollow out loaf to within about 1½ to 2 inches (3.8 - 5 cm) of crust; save excess bread.

■ Combine cream cheese, mayonnaise, beer, lime juice, hot pepper sauce and garlic salt. Mix well in medium bowl.

■ Fold clams into mixture. Pour clam mixture into hollowed out bread bowl and cover with bread top. Wrap loaf in foil.

■ Bake for 3 hours.

■ Use leftover bread from inside loaf to make bread cubes to dip. Lightly toast bread cubes in same oven as dip during last 5 minutes of baking time. Serves 8 to 10.

Beer-Cheese Pretzels and Dip

Beer-Cheese Pretzels:

1 (16 ounce) package bread roll mix with yeast 455 g
1 cup shredded sharp cheddar cheese   115 g
1 (12 ounce) can beer, divided, room
     temperature   355 ml
1 egg, beaten
1 tablespoon kosher salt   15 ml

■ Preheat oven to 350° (175° C).

■ Combine bread roll mix and cheddar cheese in medium bowl. Heat 1 cup (250 ml) beer to almost boiling, stir into bread mixture.

■ Add egg; mix and knead by hand for 5 minutes.

■ Let dough stand for 5 minutes; roll into desired shape. Sprinkle with kosher salt. Bake for 25 minutes or until golden brown

Dip:

1 (8 ounce) package cream cheese, softened   225 g
1 (8 ounce) package Velveeta® cheese, cubed   225 g
¾ teaspoon garlic powder   4 ml

■ Blend cream cheese and Velveeta® cheese in blender with garlic powder and remaining beer. Refrigerate until ready to serve. Serve with baked pretzels. Serves 6 to 8.

Mozzarella Hiccup Sticks

1½ cups baking mix	180 g
1 cup beer	250 ml
1 egg white	
1 (16 ounce) package mozzarella sticks	455 g
Oil	

- Mix flour with pinch of salt and pepper and slowly pour beer into flour while whisking briskly. Mix well, cover and let stand for 1 to 2 hours.

- Heat oil in deep fryer to 375° (190° C).

- Whisk egg white into batter. Dip mozzarella sticks into batter. Roll sticks well in batter and use slotted spoon to carefully lower battered mozzarella sticks into hot oil.

- Cook several at a time, remove after they turn golden brown and drain on paper towels. Serve immediately. Serves 4 to 6.

 Barley is the cereal grain used in the grist to make the mash used in the brewing of beer.

Best-Yet Fried Onion Rings

1½ cups flour	180 g
½ teaspoon baking powder	2 ml
1¼ cups beer	310 ml
3 onions, peeled	
Vegetable oil	

■ Combine flour, baking powder and ½ teaspoon (2 ml) each of salt and pepper. Gently stir in beer and mix well until batter is smooth and creamy.

■ Cut onions into ½-inch (1.2 cm) slices and separate into rings. Dredge in batter until evenly coated. Carefully drop into deep fryer with hot oil.

■ Fry until golden on both sides. Drain on paper towels.

■ Keep warm in oven at 250° (120° C) until all onion rings are fried. Serves 4.

We old folks have to find our cushions and pillows in our tankards. Strong beer is the milk of the old.

—Martin Luther

Garlic-Flavored Onion Rings

2 cups flour	240 g
2 teaspoons garlic powder	10 ml
1 egg, beaten	
1 cup beer	250 ml
3 large onions, sliced, separated into rings	
Oil	

■ Combine flour with garlic powder and a little salt and pepper. Add egg and slowly pour in beer, a little at a time, while whisking. Use just enough beer to form thick batter.

■ Heat oil in deep fryer to 375° (190° C).

■ Coat onion rings with batter and carefully place in hot oil. Cook until onions are golden brown. Remove from oil, drain on paper towels and serve immediately. Serves 4 to 5.

Bad men live that they may eat and drink, whereas good men eat and drink that they may live.

—Socrates

Batter-Fried Veggies

2 cups flour, divided	240 g
1½ cups beer	375 ml
2 eggs, slightly beaten	
1 cup milk	250 ml
1 zucchini, cut into 2-inch (5 cm) thin strips	
1 onion, sliced into rings	
6 fresh mushrooms, stems removed	
Vegetable oil	

■ Combine 1½ cups (180 g) flour and beer in medium bowl and mix. Let stand at room temperature for 3 hours.

■ Combine eggs and milk in separate bowl. In third bowl, mix remaining flour and ½ teaspoon salt.

■ Dip each vegetable in egg-milk mixture; then in flour-salt mixture and finally dip each vegetable in beer-flour mixture. Carefully place each vegetable in deep fryer with hot oil and fry until golden brown. Drain on paper towels and serve immediately. Serves 4.

TIP: Other vegetables, such as carrots, cauliflower, broccoli, etc., can also be fried.

 The Pabst Brewing Company was started by Jacob Best in Milwaukee in 1844.

Beer-Battered Chicken Strips

Batter:

1 (12 ounce) bottle Blatz® beer	355 ml
1½ cups flour	180 g
1 teaspoon seasoned salt	5 ml
2 eggs, beaten	

Honey-Mustard Dipping Sauce:

¾ cup honey	255 g
¼ cup dijon-style mustard	60 g
¼ cup mayonnaise	55g

1 pound chicken breast tenders	455 g
Oil	

■ Combine beer, eggs and seasoned salt in bowl. Stir in flour and add more if needed to make thin batter. Refrigerate batter for 1 to 2 hours.

■ Prepare dipping sauce by blending honey, mustard and mayonnaise; refrigerate.

■ Heat oil in deep fryer to 350° (175° C). Stir batter well and coat each chicken strip with batter. Carefully place chicken in hot oil and fry for about 2 minutes. Turn once and fry until both sides are golden brown. Serve with dipping sauce. Serves 2 to 3 as main dish; serves 6 to 8 as appetizer.

Wobbly Woasted Wings

3 - 3½ pounds chicken wings	1.4 - 1.6 kg
1 cup light beer	250 ml
½ cup light soy sauce	125 ml
½ cup extra-virgin olive oil	125 ml
¼ cup lemon juice	60 ml
2 - 6 cloves garlic, minced	
Hot sauce, optional	

■ Wash, drain and pat dry chicken wings. Mix all ingredients except chicken wings in 9 x 13-inch (23 x 33 cm) glass baking dish.

■ Add chicken to baking dish or pour marinade into large plastic bag with chicken and seal. Coat thoroughly and refrigerate overnight. Turn several times to get marinade on chicken.

■ Preheat oven to 350° (175° C).

■ Place wings skin side up in sprayed large roasting pan. Discard marinade. Roast for about 1 hour or until golden brown. Serves 6 to 10.

Attracting more than half a million people each year, Oktoberfest Zinzinnati (Cincinnati, Ohio) is the largest Oktoberfest in the United States.

Spicy Brown Ale Wings

4 pounds chicken wings	1.8 kg
½ cup packed brown sugar	110 g
½ cup kosher salt	60 g
2 (12 ounce) bottles brown ale	2 (355 ml)
1 cup (2 sticks) butter	230 g
2 - 3 cloves garlic, minced	
½ - 1 cup hot pepper sauce	125 - 250 ml
1 teaspoon finely ground black pepper	1 ml

■ Trim small tips off wings and discard. Separate remaining 2 parts of wings. Rinse, drain and pat dry with paper towels.

■ Mix brown sugar, salt and ale in large bowl and whisk until sugar and salt dissolve. Place wings in bowl and stir to coat. Cover and refrigerate for 4 to 8 hours.

■ Melt butter in large skillet and saute garlic until translucent. Add hot pepper sauce and ground black pepper. Mix well and simmer for 3 minutes.

■ Remove wings from marinade, drain on paper towels and pat dry. Discard marinade. Grill over indirect heat until brown and crispy.

■ Turn wings and brush on butter-garlic mixture during cooking process. Pour any remaining butter mixture over wings before serving. Serves about 6 to 8 as main dish; serves 12 to 16 as appetizer.

Killer Kielbasa Bites

1½ (12 ounce) cans light beer	1½ (355 ml)
1 (18 ounce) bottle barbecue sauce	510 g
½ cup packed brown sugar	110 g
¼ cup Dijon-style mustard	60 g
1 tablespoon lemon juice	15 ml
1 teaspoon onion powder	5 ml
¼ teaspoon garlic powder	2 ml
2 pounds kielbasa sausage, sliced	910 g

■ Mix all ingredients, except kielbasa, in large skillet.

■ Heat sauce over medium heat; add kielbasa and cook for about 1 hour. Serve immediately. Serves 6 to 8 as appetizers.

Everybody has to believe in something... I believe I'll have another drink.
—W.C. Fields

Clam Bites

½ cup fine breadcrumbs	60 g
¼ cup minced onion	40 g
3 - 4 cloves garlic, minced	
1 tablespoon minced parsley	15 ml
½ cup (1 stick) butter, softened	115 g
¼ cup beer	60 g
4 (6 ounce) cans minced clams, drained, set aside liquid	4 (170 g)
36 baguette slices, toasted	
½ cup grated cup parmesan cheese	50 g

■ Preheat oven to 350° (175° C).

■ Mix breadcrumbs, onion, garlic, parsley and a little salt and pepper in medium bowl.

■ Stir in butter and slowly pour in beer, a little at a time, while stirring. Mixture should reach spreading consistency.

■ Stir in minced clams and mix spread well. If spread gets a little dry, add clam liquid or a little more beer.

■ Spread clam mixture on each baguette slice and place on sprayed baking sheet. Bake for about 10 minutes. Remove from oven and sprinkle parmesan cheese on top.

■ Brown under broiler until cheese melts and turns slightly golden brown. Serve hot. Serves 10 to 12.

Crazy Crab Bites

12 large mild jalapeno peppers*	
1 (6 ounce) can crabmeat	170 g
1 egg, hard-boiled, mashed	
¼ cup minced onion	40 g
¼ cup minced celery	25 g
¼ cup mayonnaise	55 g
½ (8 ounce) package cream cheese, softened	½ (225 g)
½ cup flour	690 g
¾ cup Corona® beer	125 ml
Oil	

■ Split each jalapeno lengthwise, but leave stem in place. Remove seeds and membranes. Place in skillet and simmer about 20 minutes. Remove from skillet, drain and pat dry.

■ Mix crabmeat, egg, onion, celery and mayonnaise; blend in cream cheese. Stuff cream cheese filling into each jalapeno and close tightly.

■ Cover and refrigerate for as much as 24 hours.

■ Place flour in bowl and slowly pour beer, a little at a time, into flour while stirring. Mix well to make batter consistency. Roll jalapenos in batter and set aside for about 30 minutes.

■ Heat oil to 375° (190° C). Carefully place battered jalapenos into hot oil. Fry until golden brown, drain and serve immediately. Serves 12.

TIP: Wear rubber gloves when handling jalapenos.

Spicy Beer Mussels

3 dozen mussels	
1 (12 ounce) can lager*	355 ml
2 bay leaves	
3 whole cloves	
1 teaspoon mustard seeds	5 ml
¼ teaspoon cayenne pepper	2 ml
½ lemon, sliced	
Melted butter	

- Scrub and wash mussels well on the outside in cold water. Pour beer into large soup pot and heat almost to boiling.

- Add bay leaves, cloves, mustard seeds, cayenne, lemon slices and ½ teaspoon salt. Cover and heat mixture for several minutes, but do not boil.

- Add mussels, cover and cook over medium-high heat for 5 to 10 minutes or until shells open. Remove from beer, drain and discard shells that do not open. Serve with melted butter. Serve as appetizer for 6 to 8 or as main course for 4.

TIP: Lager is a light-colored, golden, clear beer that is most popular in the United States.

 Carbonation in beer cleanses the palate better than wine.

Beer Buzz

1 ounce coffee liqueur   30 ml
7 ounces lager   205 ml

■ Pour liqueur and lager into glass and serve. Serves 1.

Black Velvet

⅓ (12 ounce) bottle Guinness® Draught beer   ⅓ (355 ml)
4 ounces champagne   125 ml

■ Pour Guinness® into glass and pour champagne on top of
     beer. Serves 1.

*Not all chemicals are bad.
Without chemicals such as hydrogen
and oxygen, for example, there
would be no way to make water,
a vital ingredient in beer.*

—Dave Barry

Brewsky Sangria

2 Bartlett pears, peeled, chopped
1 cup plus 2 tablespoons fresh lemon
     juice, divided   250 ml/30 ml
4 (12 ounce) bottles or cans lager, chilled   4 (355 ml)
1 cup triple sec   250 ml
1 (1 liter) bottle sangria
2 Bosc pears, sliced

■ Puree Bartlett pears with 2 tablespoons (30 ml) lemon juice in blender. Slowly pour beer into chilled pitcher. Add remaining 1 cup (250 ml) lemon juice, triple sec and pear puree.

■ Fill pitcher with sangria and stir well. Fill chilled pint (500 ml) glasses halfway with ice and pour sangria in glasses. Add Bosc pear slices as garnish. Serves 12.

The roots and herbes beaten and put into new ale or beer and daily drunk, cleareth, strengtheneth and quickeneth the sight of the eyes.

—Nicholas Culpeper, 17th century
English herbalist and physician

Flaming Doctor Pepper I

Shooter time – so hold on.

1 cup beer	250 ml
1 ounce amaretto liqueur	30 ml
¼ ounce 151-proof rum	7 ml

■ Pour beer into pint glass. (It will be half full.) Pour amaretto to within ¼-inch (6 mm) of top of shot glass.

■ Pour 151-proof rum on top of amaretto to fill shot glass. Light 151-proof rum with open flame.

■ Carefully drop flaming shot glass into pint glass with beer and drink as a shooter. Serves 1.

Flaming Doctor Pepper II

2 ounces amaretto liqueur	60 ml
½ ounce 151-proof rum	15 ml
1 (1½ ounce) jigger beer	45 ml

■ Pour amaretto into highball glass. Pour 151-proof rum over back of spoon into highball glass so rum stays on top of amaretto.

■ Fill shot glass with beer. Light rum with open flame. Before flame dies down, drop shot glass into flaming highball glass.

■ Beer will foam up slightly and flame will go out. Drink like a shooter. Serves 1.

TIP: You can substitute Kahlua® liqueur for amaretto for a different take on the same drink.

German-Cherry Beer

½ cup cherry juice   125 ml
1 (12 ounce) bottle or can German beer   355 ml

■   Pour cherry juice into 1 (16 ounce/500 ml) glass and pour
      in beer. Serves 1.

Ginger Shandies

3 (12 ounce) bottles Hoegaarden Original
      White ale   3 (355 ml)
1 (12 ounce) bottle ginger beer, chilled   355 ml
1 lemon, thinly sliced

■   Pour Hoegaarden ale and ginger beer into large pitcher.
      Drop lemon slices in pitcher and stir gently. Pour mixture
      into 6 ice-filled glasses and serve immediately. Serves 6.

*The aluminum can was introduced by Coors
of Golden, Colorado in 1959. The tab top was
introduced by Pittsburgh Brewing Company in
1962. The ring-pull tab was introduced in 1965.*

Granny Smacker

1 (12 ounce) bottle or can beer	355 ml
1 (6 ounce) can frozen lemonade concentrate, thawed	175 ml
2 tablespoons vodka	30 ml

■ Pour beer, lemonade and vodka into ice-filled glass, stir and serve immediately. Serves 1.

Half and Half
(aka Black & Tan)

½ (12 ounce) bottle Harp® lager	½ (355 ml)
½ (12 ounce) bottle Guinness® Draught beer	½ (355 ml)

■ Pour Harp® lager into pint glass. Pour Guinness® over back of spoon into same glass. Serves 1.

It is a fair wind that blew men to the ale.

—Oscar Wilde

Hop, Skip and Go Naked

6 (12 ounce) bottles or cans beer   6 (355 ml)
1 (12 ounce) can frozen lemonade
   concentrate   355 ml
1 pint whiskey   475 ml

- Combine beer, lemonade concentrate and whiskey in
  1-gallon pitcher and stir. Pour into ice-filled glasses.
  Serves 12.

Hot Shot Beer Cocktail

1 lime, quartered
1 - 2 dashes hot sauce
1 (12 ounce) bottle Corona beer, chilled   355 ml

- Pour salt on small saucer. Rub rim of beer mug with lime
  wedge. Turn mug upside down and press rim into salt.

- Squeeze juice of 2 lime wedges into glass. Add 1 or
  2 dashes hot sauce and pinch of salt. Pour beer into glass,
  garnish with lime wedge and serve immediately. Serves 1.

 *"All malt" refers to beer made exclusively with
barley malt and without adjuncts.*

Dandy Beer

1 (12-ounce) bottle lemon soda	355 ml
1 (12-ounce) bottle or can lager	355 ml
Lemon slices	

- Pour lemon soda and lager beer into large pitcher filled with ice. Stir well and serve in chilled glasses. Garnish with lemon slices. Serves 2.

Irish Black Russian

1½ ounces coffee-flavored liqueur, cold	45 ml
3 ounces vodka, cold	90 ml
1 (12 ounce) bottle or can Irish stout, cold	355 ml
1 (8 ounce) can Coke®, cold	235 ml

- Pour coffee liqueur and vodka into 3 highball glasses. Pour Coke® in same glasses to within ½ inch (1.2 cm) of top. Pour Irish stout to form foam on top. Serve as is or stir. Serves 3.

He was a wise man who invented beer.
—Plato

Irish Car Bomb I

1 (12 ounce) bottle or can Irish stout	355 ml
1 (1½ ounce) jigger Irish whiskey	45 ml

■ Pour Irish stout into beer mug. Drop jigger of whiskey into beer mug and let it sink to bottom. Drink beer all at once including jigger of whiskey. Serves 1.

Irish Car Bomb II

½ (12 ounce) bottle or can Irish stout	½ (355 ml)
¾ ounce Irish whiskey	22 ml
¾ ounce Irish cream liqueur	22 ml

■ Pour Irish stout into beer mug. Pour Irish whiskey and Irish cream liqueur into 1½-ounce jigger.

■ Drop jigger of whiskey and Irish cream into beer mug and let it sink to bottom. Drink beer all at once including whiskey and Irish cream. Serves 1.

 Beer is any beverage that contains alcohol produced by fermenting grain, specifically malt, and flavored with hops.

Lime Beer Cocktail

6 (12 ounce) bottles or cans light beer, chilled 6 (355 ml)
1 (6 ounce) can frozen limeade concentrate   175 ml
1 lime, halved

■ Pour beer into chilled pitcher and slowly stir in frozen limeade. Allow foam to settle.

■ Squeeze ½ lime into pitcher. Slice remaining ½ lime and drop into pitcher. Pour beer into chilled glasses and serve immediately. Serves 6.

Beer Margaritas

2 (12 ounce) cans frozen lemonade
    concentrate   2 (355 ml)
1½ cups vodka   355 ml
2 (12 ounce) bottles or cans beer   2 (355 ml)

■ Mix lemonade concentrate, vodka and beer in large pitcher. Pour into chilled, ice-filled glasses. Serves 8.

WOODY: How would a beer feel,
         Mr. Peterson?
NORM: Pretty nervous if I was
        in the room.
                —Cheers

Frozen Beer Margaritas

Margarita salt	
1 lime, sliced	
1 (12 ounce) can frozen limeade concentrate	355 ml
½ (12 ounce) bottle or can beer	½ (355 ml)
6 ounces tequila	175 ml

■ Pour salt in small saucer. Press lime slices around rims of 2 margarita glasses. Turn glasses upside down and press into salt.

■ Pour limeade concentrate, beer and tequila in blender and fill to top with ice. Blend until smooth and pour into margarita glasses. Garnish with lime slice. Serves 2.

Did you know that the word "toddlers" originated in England and was used to describe babies who were given beer instead water to drink? Beer was not only more nutritious, but safer to drink than the water.

Mexicali Margaritas

1 (12 ounce) can limeade concentrate	355 ml
1½ cups gold tequila	355 ml
3 (12 ounce) cans Mexican beer	3 (355 ml)
1 lime, quartered	

■ Pour limeade concentrate, tequila and beer into chilled pitcher and stir. Pour margarita into ice-filled glasses. Squeeze lemon wedge into each glass and drop on top for garnish. Serves 8.

Whiskey's too rough,
Champagne costs too much,
Vodka puts my mouth in gear.
I hope this refrain,
Will help me explain,
As a matter of fact, I like beer.

—Tom T. Hall, country music singer

Nova Scotia Beer Warmer

1 (12 ounce) bottle or can beer   355 ml
3 dashes hot pepper sauce

■   Pour beer into mug and add several dashes hot sauce.
Serve immediately. Serves 1.

Orange Beer Burst

1 ounce orange liqueur   30 ml
7 ounces lager   205 ml

■   Pour orange liqueur and lager into glass and stir.
Serves 1.

Microbreweries produce their own flavors and styles of beer and package it primarily for local consumption. Generally, they may be defined as breweries that produce small quantities of very high quality, traditional-style beers.

Red Eye

7 ounces lager	205 ml
1 ounce tomato juice	30 ml
Dash hot sauce	
Juice of 1 lemon	
Juice of 1 lime	

■ Pour lager into glass and add remaining ingredients. Serves 1.

Shady Leprechaun

1½ ounces dark rum	45 ml
1 (1 pint) bottle Irish stout	475 ml

■ Pour rum into pint glass. Slowly pour in stout. Serves 4 leprechauns or 1 human.

Always do sober what you said you'd do drunk. That will teach you to keep your mouth shut.
—Ernest Hemingway

Shandy

1 (12 ounce) bottle or can lager	355 ml
½ cup lemonade	125 ml

■ Pour cold beer into beer mug and slowly pour in cold lemonade. Stir a little. Serves 1.

Spicy Beer Mary

Celery salt	
1 lemon, quartered	
2 (12-ounce) bottles or cans lager	2 (355 ml)
1 (12 ounce) can spicy vegetable juice	355 ml
Worcestershire sauce	
Freshly ground black pepper	
2 ribs celery	

■ Pour celery salt on small saucer. Rub edges of 2 (16 ounce/500 ml) beer mugs with lemon wedge, turn upside down and press into salt.

■ Fill mugs with ice. Pour half beer into each mug and top with spicy vegetable juice.

■ Add several dashes of Worcestershire and pepper. Garnish with remaining lemon wedges and celery ribs. Serves 2.

Spicy Red Beer

1 (6 ounce) can tomato juice	175 ml
Hot sauce	
Worcestershire sauce	
1 (12 ounce) bottle or can beer	355 ml

■ Pour tomato juice and a dash or two of hot sauce and Worcestershire sauce in chilled beer mug. Add pinch of salt and pour beer on top. Stir and serve. Serves 1.

Dirty Spicy Red Beer

½ cup tomato juice	125 ml
Hot sauce	
Worcestershire sauce	
Splash olive juice	
1 (12 ounce) bottle pale ale	355 ml
Pimento-stuffed olive	

■ Pour tomato juice and a dash or two of hot sauce and Worcestershire sauce in beer mug. Add dash or two of olive juice and pour beer on top.

■ Drop pimento-stuffed olive into glass and serve immediately. Serves 1.

Snakebite

½ pint Harp lager   235 ml
½ pint pear cider   235 ml

■ Pour ingredients into a pint (500 ml) glass. Serves 1.

Summer Beer

1 (6 ounce) can frozen lemonade concentrate 175 ml
1 (12 ounce) bottle or can beer   355 ml
1½ cups vodka   375 ml

■ Crush 4 cups (1 L) ice in blender. Add lemonade
concentrate, beer and vodka and blend until smooth.
Pour into chilled glasses. Serves 8.

*New York and Pennsylvania accounted for 85% of
the beer brewed in the U.S. in 1860. There were
more than 1200 breweries producing over one
million barrels of beer annually.*

Soups
&
Breads

Traditional Clambakes
and Clamboils

*Beach parties are enjoyed around the world.
The beach is the perfect setting for celebrations
and fun with ice cold beer. No other beverage,
outside of water, has the same popularity
and common use at celebrations as beer.*

Traditional Clambakes and Clamboils

Clambake at the Beach, Clambake in the Backyard and Clamboil in the Kitchen

It doesn't matter where you have a clambake or clamboil, the important thing is to just do it. There are few celebrations better for beer than clambakes and clamboils.

The secret to any great clambake or clamboil is to use local seafood and fresh seaweed. If you're not close to a beach, get seaweed from a local fresh seafood market or substitute spinach soaked in salted water.

Menu for 10 to 12 people:

2 - 3 pounds (910 g - 1.4 kg) clams, steamers or mussels
Fresh seaweed or rockweed
6 - 8 (1½ pound/680 g) lobsters
8 - 10 ears corn-on-the-cob in shucks, silks removed
10 - 12 red potatoes

Clambake at the Beach

■ Wash clams, steamers or mussels to remove sand. Wash about 3 to 5 pounds (1.4 to 2.3 kg) seaweed or rockweed to remove sand and soak in salt water to keep fresh.

■ Dig large hole in sand about 2 to 3 feet (60 to 90 cm) deep and about 3 to 4 feet (90 cm to 1.2 m) wide. Line bottom of hole with smooth, non-porous rocks that will hold the heat.

Continued next page...

Continued from previous page...

■ Build wood fire on top of rocks and burn until there are enough hot coals to heat rocks to a temperature of 400° (205° C). (This will take several hours with a roaring fire.) Rocks are ready when water droplets sizzle and spit when they land on the rocks. Rake ashes of fire between rocks and to the sides.

■ Layer wet seaweed over heated stones. Place layer of lobster, layer of seaweed, layer of potatoes, another layer of seaweed, corn and clams with several inches of wet seaweed on top. If you want to contain the food more, wrap it in cheesecloth bundles, lay on seaweed and place remaining seaweed on top.

■ Cover hole, food and seaweed with wet canvas tarp. Anchor edges of tarp with rocks to seal and hold in the steam. Steam food for about 2 hours or until clam shells open and lobsters turn bright red. Serve with lots of melted butter and bibs.

Clambake in the Backyard

■ Clambakes work great in a backyard using the family grill. Wash clams, steamers or mussels to remove sand. Wash about 2 to 3 pounds (910 to 1.4 kg) seaweed or rockweed to remove sand and soak in salt water to keep fresh.

■ Wrap lobsters, clams and corn in cheesecloth with a little seaweed and tie into about 8 to 10 bundles. Wrap each bundle in foil tightly and place on grill over charcoal or gas fire. Steam food in packages for about 1 hour or until clams open and corn is tender.

Continued next page...

Continued from previous page...

TIP: You can grill oysters, clams and mussels directly over a charcoal fire, but you must wash beards off the shells or they will catch on fire. Place the shells over the fire with the cup side facing up so juices won't run out. Serve when shells open. Discard any unopened shells. Serve with lots of melted butter.

Clamboil in the Kitchen

■ Wash clams, steamers or mussels to remove sand. Wash about 2 to 3 pounds (910 g to 1.4 kg) seaweed or rockweed to remove sand. Divide it into 4 equal piles.

■ Pour about 2 inches of water into 20-quart (20 L) stock pot. Put one pile of seaweed into pot with water. Add lobsters and second layer of seaweed. Add corn and potatoes and another layer of seaweed. Add clams. mussels and remaining seaweed.

■ Cover pot, bring water to a boil, reduce heat to low and steam for 30 to 45 minutes or until clams open. Discard any clams or mussels that do not open. Serve on platters with lots of melted butter and your favorite beverages.

TIP: If you can't find seaweed anywhere, substitute spinach soaked in salted water. It'll work.

Check out these great recipes for clambakes, clamboils or just plain fun.

Easy Cheese Soup

¼ cup (½ stick) butter	55 g
¼ cup flour	30 g
1 (1 pint) carton half-and-half cream	500 ml
1 (12 ounce) can beer (not light)	355 ml
1 (16 ounce) package cubed Velveeta® cheese	455 g
¼ teaspoon cayenne pepper	1 ml
2 teaspoons marinade for chicken*	2 ml

■ Melt butter in large soup pot, add flour and stir until smooth. Cook for 1 minute. Gradually add half-and-half cream and beer and cook over medium heat, stirring constantly, until thick.

■ Add cheese and stir until cheese melts. Stir in cayenne pepper, marinade for chicken, and a little salt and pepper, if you like. Heat while stirring and ladle into soup bowls. (Don't let liquid boil or beer will turn bitter.) Serves 6.

TIP: Marinade for chicken is a light-colored version of Worcestershire sauce.

*Wine is but single broth,
ale is meat, drink and cloth.*
—16th century English proverb

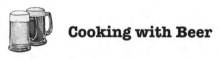

Creamy Dreamy Cheese Soup

½ cup (1 stick) butter	115 g
½ cup flour	60 g
4 cups milk or half-and-half cream	1 L
3 (16 ounce) packages shredded sharp cheddar cheese	3 (455 g)
1 (16 ounce) package shredded carrots	455 g
1 onion, minced	
1 teaspoon garlic powder	5 ml
1 (14 ounce) can chicken broth	395 g
2 (10 ounce) cans cream of chicken soup	2 (280 g)
1½ (12 ounce) bottles or cans light beer	1½ (355 ml)
1 tablespoon dijon-style mustard	15 ml
2 teaspoons Worcestershire sauce	10 ml
1 teaspoon hot sauce	5 ml

■ Melt butter in large soup pot. Add flour, stir constantly to remove lumps and cook for about 3 minutes. Slowly pour in milk or half-and-half cream and continue to stir. (Do not scorch milk.)

■ Continue stirring until mixture thickens. Remove from heat, add cheese and stir until cheese melts.

■ Place carrots, onion, garlic powder, chicken broth and soup in large saucepan and heat over medium-high heat. Add beer, mustard and Worcestershire and stir well to mix.

■ Pour carrot mixture into soup pot with cheese and stir well. Serve hot. Serves 8 to 10.

Buttery Cheddar Soup

½ cup (1 stick) butter	115 g
6 green onions with tops, minced	
1 red bell pepper, seeded, minced	
1 bay leaf	
½ cup flour	60 g
¾ cup beer, divided	175 ml
2 (14 ounce) cans chicken broth	2 (395 g)
1 cup whipping cream	250 ml
1 (8 ounce) package shredded cheddar cheese	225 g

■ Melt butter in large saucepan and cook onions and bell pepper until onions are translucent. Add bay leaf and about ½ teaspoon salt and stir.

■ Add flour and a little beer and stir until flour is creamy and has no lumps. Add remaining beer, broth and cream and cook until mixture is steaming, but not boiling.

■ Add cheese and stir constantly until cheese melts. Taste and adjust seasonings if needed. Serves 6 to 8.

If you want to thicken soups or stews after adding beer, use dry potato flakes. Sprinkle several tablespoons into liquid and cook on low for five to ten minutes. Add more potato flakes if needed.

Hefe Proper Cheese Soup

½ cup (1 stick) butter	115 g
½ cup flour	60 g
5 cups milk	1.2 L
2 cups Hefe Proper	500 ml
1 tablespoon Worcestershire sauce	15 ml
1 teaspoon mustard	5 ml
½ teaspoon cayenne pepper	2 ml
1 (16 ounce) package shredded cheddar cheese	455 g

■ Melt butter in large saucepan over medium heat. Add flour, stir constantly for about 1 minute and stir out lumps.

■ Reduce heat to low and add milk, Hefe Proper, Worcestershire, mustard, cayenne and ½ teaspoon (5 ml) salt. Add cheese and stir constantly until cheese melts. Serves 4.

 Anheuser-Busch bought the St. Louis Cardinals baseball team in 1953.

Black Bean Beer Soup

2 (14 ounce) cans beef broth	2 (395 g)
1 (12 ounce) bottle or can lager	355 ml
1 cup pico de gallo salsa	130 g
½ cup instant black bean soup mix	125 ml
3 green onions with tops, minced	
⅓ cup chopped yellow bell pepper	50 g
⅓ cup shredded queso fresco, optional	45 g

■ Heat broth, beer and salsa on medium-low in large saucepan. Reduce heat to low, stir in soup mix, white part of onions and bell peppers and cook for 10 to 15 minutes.

■ Pour into soup mugs, garnish with green tops of onions and cheese and serve. Serves 4.

*Make sure that the beer —
four pints a week — goes to the
troops under fire before any of
the parties in the rear get a drop.*
—Winston Churchill
to his Secretary of War, 1944

Quick Cream of Potato Soup

2 tablespoons butter	30 g
1 medium onion, minced	
2 cooked ham steak slices, chopped	
1 cup nonfat dry milk powder	70 g
1 (14 ounce) can chicken broth	395 g
2 (12 ounce) bottles or cans beer, room	
temperature	2 (355 ml)
1 cup instant potato flakes	60 g

■ Melt butter in soup pot and cook onion until translucent. Add ham and cook over low heat about 5 minutes.

■ Add dry milk powder and chicken broth and cook over low heat. When mixture is hot, add beer and potato flakes and remove from heat. Stir to mix well. Serve immediately. Serves 4.

Don't boil soups and stews after you add beer. The beer will turn bitter and ruin a dish. If a savory dish turns bitter from the beer, add sauteed, cooked carrots, a little lemon juice and extra spices.

French Onion Soup

⅓ cup (⅔ stick) butter	75 g
10 onions, peeled, chopped	
2 cloves garlic, minced	
1 (12 ounce) bottle or can beer	355 ml
2 (14 ounce) cans beef broth	2 (395 g)
½ teaspoon dry mustard	2 ml
1 bay leaf	
6 slices French bread, toasted	
3 cups shredded gruyere cheese	340 g

- Melt butter in large saucepan and saute onions and garlic until translucent.

- Add beer, broth, mustard and bay leaf to saucepan and cook on high just until mixture is hot. (Do not boil.)

- Reduce heat to low, cover and cook for about 30 minutes.

- Pour soup into ovenproof soup mugs. Place toasted bread slice on top and cover with cheese.

- Place mugs on baking sheet and warm in oven at 250° (120° C) until cheese melts. Serves 4 to 6.

SAM: What d'you like, Normie?
NORM: A reason to live. Give
me another beer.
—Cheers

German Summer Soup

¼ cup oil	60 ml
1 pound beef stew meat, cubed	455 g
1 onion, chopped	
1 tablespoon paprika	15 ml
¼ teaspoon caraway seeds	1 ml
1 (12 ounce) bottle or can beer	355 ml
½ (6 ounce) can tomato paste	½ (170 g)
5 red potatoes, quartered	
2 ounces sauerkraut	55 g

■ Heat oil in large heavy skillet over medium-high heat and brown stew meat to remove all pink color. Add onion and cook until translucent.

■ Add paprika, caraway seeds, and about ¼ teaspoon (1 ml) each of salt and pepper. Pour in beer and about ¾ cup (175 ml) water. Cover and cook on low for about 1 hour.

■ Add tomato paste, potatoes and sauerkraut (don't drain) and cook until potatoes are tender. Cook additional 10 to 15 minutes to reduce liquid. Serve immediately. Serves 4.

The first beer from a "microbrewery" was served in Sonoma, California in 1977.

Newcastle Stew & Dumplings

2 pounds beef chuck roast, cubed	910 g
¼ cup flour	30 g
Canola oil	
3 slices bacon, chopped	
4 potatoes, peeled, quartered	
3 carrots, sliced	
3 ribs celery, sliced	
2 large onions, chopped	
2 tablespoons rosemary	30 ml
3 (12 ounce) bottles or cans Newcastle	
dark ale	3 (355 ml)

■ Season beef with a little salt and pepper and coat all sides with flour. Heat oil in large soup pot over medium-high heat and brown beef. Remove beef and set aside. Fry bacon until half cooked.

■ Return beef to soup pot. Add potatoes, carrots, celery, onions, rosemary and a little salt and pepper. Pour ale and 1 cup (250 ml) water into soup pot and cook on medium for about 1 hour. (Do not boil.) Add water if needed.

Dumplings:

1¾ cups flour	210 g
½ cup (1 stick) butter, softened	115 g

■ Mix flour and butter and add a little water to make dough consistency. Form into golf ball-size dumplings and drop into soup. Cover pot and cook for additional 2 hours.

■ Taste for seasonings and serve hot. Serves 6 to 8.

Simple Beef Stew

¼ cup oil	60 g
2 - 3 pounds stew meat	910 g - 1.4 kg
1 large onion, chopped	
2 ribs celery, minced	
1 (12 ounce) bottle or can beer	355 ml
½ teaspoon seasoned pepper	2 ml
½ teaspoon dried thyme	2 ml
1 (16 ounce) package frozen stew vegetables	455 g

■ Pour oil into large stew pot over medium-high heat. Add stew meat and brown on all sides. Reduce heat, cover and cook for about 10 minutes.

■ Add onion, celery, beer, seasoned pepper, thyme and salt to taste and cook covered over low heat for about 20 minutes.

■ Add frozen vegetables and cook uncovered until done. Serve immediately. Serves 8 to 10.

Did you know that beer advanced science in the early 1670's when Anton van Leeuwenhoek, a Dutch scientist, discovered yeast by peering through his microscope at beer?

Easy Dutch Oven Stew

3 pounds beef stew meat	1.4 kg
1 tablespoon lemon pepper	15 ml
1 teaspoon thyme	5 ml
¼ cup oil	60 ml
2 (14 ounce) cans beef broth	2 (395 g)
1 (12 ounce) bottle or can beer	355 ml
3 large potatoes, peeled, quartered	
3 large carrots, peeled, quartered	
3 large onions, peeled, quartered	
3 bay leaves	

■ Season stew meat with lemon pepper, thyme and 1 teaspoon (5 ml) salt. Place in Dutch oven or large soup pot with oil and brown on all sides over medium-high heat.

■ Reduce heat to medium and pour broth and beer into pot. (Do not allow beer to boil.) Add potatoes, carrots, onions, bay leaves and 1 teaspoon (1 ml) pepper.

■ Cook stew covered on medium heat for about 1 hour to 1 hour 30 minutes or until beef is done and vegetables are tender. Add more beer or broth if needed to keep stew meat covered. Serves 8.

There may be a few good men who don't drink, but they've got to prove it.
–Col. Lincoln Karmany, USMC

Guinness Stew

2 pounds beef chuck roast, cubed	910 g
1 tablespoon flour	15 ml
¼ cup oil	60 ml
1 large onion, chopped	
4 cloves garlic, minced	
3 carrots, chopped	
6 new potatoes, peeled, chopped	
1 tablespoon parsley flakes	15 ml
1 tablespoon tomato paste	15 ml
1 (12 ounce) bottle Guinness® Stout	355 ml
2 (14 ounce) cans beef broth	2 (395 g)

■ Sprinkle a little salt and pepper over beef and dredge in flour. Brown on all sides in hot oil in large soup pot. Saute onion and garlic in same pot until translucent.

■ Add carrots and potatoes and cook for about 5 minutes. Stir in parsley flakes, tomato paste, Guinness® and broth.

■ Cook on high, but do not boil. Reduce heat and cook, covered, on low for about 1 hour 30 minutes. Remove cover and cook for additional 30 minutes or until beef is tender. Serves 8.

 Beer is sometimes called "liquid bread" because of its yeast content.

Tomato-Beef Stew

3 pounds beef chuck roast, cubed	1.4 kg
¼ cup oil	60 ml
2 onions, chopped	
2 ribs celery, minced	
2 cloves garlic, minced	
1 (28 ounce) can diced tomatoes with liquid	795 g
1 (14 ounce) can beef broth	395 g
2 teaspoons ground cumin	10 ml
2 tablespoons Worcestershire sauce	30 ml
1 (12 ounce) bottle or can beer	355 ml

- Place beef in large roasting pan and brown in oil. Drain beef on paper towels. Saute onions, celery and garlic in same oil until translucent. Place beef back in pan.

- Add tomatoes, broth, cumin, Worcestershire, and a little salt and pepper. Bring to boil and reduce heat to low. Add beer and cook, covered, for 2 hours. (Do not allow beer to boil.)

- Uncover and cook for additional 30 to 45 minutes to reduce liquid to desired consistency. Serves 8.

The problem with the world is that everyone is a few drinks behind.
—Humphrey Bogart

Deer Camp Beer Stew

1 (28 ounce) can Mexican stewed tomatoes	795 g
1 (14 ounce) can beef broth	395 g
2 - 3 pounds venison roast, cubed	910 g - 1.4 kg
Bacon drippings or canola oil	
1 (6 ounce) bottle Worcestershire sauce	170 g
2 - 3 teaspoons paprika	10 - 15 ml
2 - 3 jalapenos, seeded, chopped*	
1 (12 ounce) bottle or can beer	355 ml
5 - 6 potatoes, chopped	
3 - 4 large onions, chopped	
1 (16 ounce) bag baby carrots, sliced	455 g
3 - 4 ribs celery, chopped	

■ Pour tomatoes and beef broth into large stew pot and turn heat to warm.

■ Brown venison in bacon drippings in large skillet. Pour venison and pan drippings into stew pot.

■ Add Worcestershire, paprika, 2 teaspoons (10 ml) each of salt and pepper, and jalapenos. Bring stew almost to a boil (but do not boil) and reduce heat to low. Add beer and cook for about 2 to 3 hours or until venison is fairly tender. Add more beer if needed.

■ Add potatoes, onions and carrots and cook on low heat for additional 1 to 2 hours. Adjust seasonings to taste as stew cooks.

■ Add celery about 15 to 20 minutes before serving to give stew a little crunch. Serves 8 to 10.

TIP: Wear rubber gloves when handling jalapenos.

TIP: Do not boil beer or it will give stew a bitter taste.

Game-Day Chili

¼ cup oil	60 ml
1 pound ground round or lean ground beef	455 g
2 pounds beef stew meat, cubed	910 g
2 large onions, chopped	
2 cloves garlic, minced	
2 (14 ounce) cans diced tomatoes	2 (395 g)
1 (6 ounce) can tomato sauce	170 g
3 (15 ounce) cans pinto beans with jalapenos	3 (425 g)
1 (12 ounce) bottle or can beer	355 ml
1 cup strong brewed coffee	250 ml
1 (14 ounce) can beef broth	395 g
¼ - ½ cup chili powder	30 - 65 g
2 tablespoons ground cumin	30 ml

■ Heat oil in large roasting pan over medium-high heat and brown ground beef until pink is gone. Repeat process for stew meat. Add onions, garlic, diced tomatoes, tomato sauce, pinto beans and stir well.

■ Pour beer, coffee, broth, chili powder, cumin and 1 teaspoon (5 ml) salt into pot, stir well and cover. Cook on low for about 1 hour.

■ Adjust seasonings, add more liquid if needed and simmer for additional 1 hour. Serves 8 to 10.

Adolphus Busch began bottling beer on a large scale at the Anheuser Brewery in St. Louis in 1873.

Cheap Beer Chili

*If you have some cheap beer around that you
don't want to drink, this is a good way to use it.*

2 tablespoons oil	30 ml
1 pound beef stew meat	455 g
1 pound ground beef	455 g
2 onions, chopped	
3 cloves garlic, minced	
1 (7 ounce) can tomato sauce	200 g
1 (7 ounce) can diced tomatoes and green chilies	200 g
2 jalapenos, seeded, minced*	
¼ cup chili powder	30 g
1 teaspoon ground cumin	5 ml
1 (12 ounce) bottle or can beer	355 ml

■ Heat oil in large skillet over medium-high heat and brown
stew meat and ground beef until all pink is gone. Add
onions and garlic and cook until translucent.

■ Add tomato sauce, tomatoes and green chilies, jalapenos,
chili powder, cumin, and a little salt and pepper. Stir
in beer and cook on low to medium, covered, for about
1 hour; stir occasionally.

■ Remove from heat and taste to adjust seasonings. Cook
for additional 20 to 30 minutes uncovered or until liquid
is consistency you want. Serves 6.

TIP: Wear rubber gloves when handling jalapenos.

Porter Black Bean Chili

1 tablespoon oil	15 ml
1 pound ground chuck roast	455 g
2 (15 ounce) cans black beans	2 (425 g)
2 onions, diced	
2 cloves garlic, minced	
2 tablespoons chili powder	30 ml
1 (15 ounce) can stewed chopped tomatoes	425 g
1 (14 ounce) can beef broth	395 g
½ cup porter	125 ml

■ Heat oil in heavy skillet over medium-high heat and brown ground beef until all pink is gone. Add a little salt and pepper and stir. (There shouldn't be much grease, but drain some if necessary.)

■ Add black beans, onions, garlic, chili powder, tomatoes, broth and porter and cook on low for about 1 hour. Liquid should reduce over cooking time. Serves 4.

For we could not now take time for further search (to land our ship), our victuals being much spent, especially our beer.

—from the log of *The Mayflower*

Ranch Venison Chili

Chase this "bowl of red" with flour
tortillas, jalapenos and a beer or two.

4 onions, minced	
¼ cup canola oil	60 ml
2 - 3 pounds venison, cubed	910 g - 1.4 kg
1 pound pork sausage or bacon, optional	455 g
1 cup light beer	250 ml
6 - 8 dried New Mexico Red chile peppers, ground	
3 - 4 jalapenos, seeded, chopped*	
2 - 3 cloves garlic, minced	
2 teaspoons paprika	10 ml
2 teaspoons ground cumin	10 ml

■ Brown onions in oil in large, heavy roasting pan until translucent.

■ Add venison, a little at a time, and brown on all sides. Sprinkle a little salt and pepper on venison as it browns. Add a little oil, if needed. Add pork sausage or bacon and brown.

■ Pour in 1 cup (250 ml) water, beer, New Mexico Reds, jalapenos, garlic, paprika and cumin and stir well.

■ Cook over medium-high heat for about 10 minutes, but do not boil. Reduce heat to low and cook for additional 2 to 3 hours. (Add 1 to 2 cups (250 to 500 ml) more water if needed for consistency desired. Adjust seasonings if water is added.)

■ Cook for additional 1 to 2 hours. Serves 8 to 10.

TIP: *Dried New Mexico Red chile peppers are great in chili. They are sweet to mild. They are found in ristras in New Mexico and Texas border towns.*

*TIP: *Wear rubber gloves when handling jalapenos.*

Vegetarian Chili

1 (14 ounce) can diced tomatoes	395 g
1 (12 ounce) can beer or 1 (14 ounce) can vegetable broth	355 ml/395 g
1 (8 ounce) can no-salt tomato sauce	230 g
2 tablespoons reduced-sodium chili seasoning mix	30 ml
2 (15 ounce) cans pinto or red kidney beans, rinsed, drained	2 (425 g)

■ Combine all ingredients and 1 cup (250 ml) water in large heavy pan. Bring almost to a boil, reduce heat and simmer uncovered for about 20 minutes. Add water if needed. Serves 4 to 5.

When we drink, we get drunk. When we get drunk, we fall asleep. When we fall asleep, we commit no sin. When we commit no sin, we go to heaven. Soooo, let's all get drunk and go to heaven!

—Brian O'Rourke

Gumbo

1 tablespoon plus 1 cup olive oil, divided	15 ml/250 ml
2 boneless, skinless chicken breast halves, chopped	
½ pound pork sausage links, thinly sliced	225 g
1 cup flour	120 g
2 tablespoons minced garlic	30 ml
2 (32 ounce) cartons chicken broth	2 (910 g)
1 (12 ounce) bottle or can beer	355 ml
5 ribs celery, diced	
1 sweet onion, sliced	
1 (10 ounce) can diced tomatoes and green chilies	280 g
¼ cup Cajun-Creole seasoning	50 g
1 pound cooked, peeled, veined shrimp	455 g
1 (16 ounce) package frozen cut okra	455 g
Cooked rice	

- Heat 1 tablespoon (15 ml) oil in large skillet over medium-high heat and cook chicken until juices run clear. Add sausage and cook to brown. Remove from skillet and drain all on paper towels.

- Pour remaining 1 cup (250 ml) olive oil into skillet over medium to medium-high heat and add flour a little at a time, stirring constantly. When mixture turns light brown, add garlic and cook for 1 minute.

- Add broth and beer a little at a time and stir after each addition. Mix in celery, onion, tomatoes and green chilies, and Cajun-Creole seasoning and cook on medium-low for about 30 minutes.

- Add chicken, sausage and shrimp and cook for about 30 minutes; stir several times. Just before serving, add okra and cook for several minutes. Serve hot over rice. Serves 8 to 10.

Easy Beer Bread

3 cups flour	360 g
1 tablespoon baking powder	15 ml
¼ cup sugar	50 g
1 (12 ounce) bottle or can beer	355 ml

■ Preheat oven to 375° (190° C).

■ Combine flour, baking powder, sugar and beer in large bowl and mix well. Pour into sprayed 9 x 5-inch (23 x 13 cm) loaf pan and bake die about 50 minutes or until top is golden brown. Yields 1 loaf.

Basic Beer Bread

3 cups flour	360 g
1 tablespoon baking powder	15 ml
3 tablespoons sugar	40 g
1 (12 ounce) bottle or can beer	355 ml
¼ cup (½ stick) butter, melted	55 g

■ Preheat oven to 350° (175° C).

■ Mix flour, baking powder, and sugar in large bowl. Add beer, a little at a time, and mix well after each addition. Pour batter into sprayed 9 x 5-inch (23 x 13 cm) loaf pan. Bake for 30 minutes.

■ Brush melted butter over bread. Bake for additional 10 minutes. Tap bottom of pan and if it sounds hollow, remove bread from pan. Brush with any remaining melted butter. Yields 1 loaf.

Beer Bread

There are lots of versions of beer bread. You will find several here, but you can add your own seasonings and additions.

4 cups flour	480 g
2 tablespoons baking powder	30 ml
¼ cup sugar	60 g
1 (12 ounce) bottle or can beer	355 ml
2 eggs, slightly beaten	

- Preheat oven to 350° (175° C).

- Mix flour, baking powder, sugar and 2 teaspoons (10 ml) salt in large bowl. Pour beer into flour mixture a little at a time. Add egg and stir well. (If the batter is too dry to stir easily, knead with hands.)

- Pour batter into sprayed 9 x 5-inch (23 x 13 cm) loaf pan. Bake for about 1 hour or until golden brown on top. Remove from pan as soon as bread comes out of oven and cool on wire rack. Yields 1 loaf.

TIP: Do not use light beer with bread recipes.

There are more breweries in the United States than any other country in the world. The popularity of "microbreweries" has created interest and patronage across the country.

Texas Beer Bread

3 cups self-rising flour	360 g
¼ cup sugar	50 g
1 (12 ounce) can beer, room temperature	355 ml
1 egg, beaten	
2 tablespoons butter, melted	30 g

- ■ Preheat oven to 350° (175° C).

- ■ Combine flour, sugar and beer in bowl and mix until they blend well. Spoon into sprayed 9 x 5-inch (23 x 13 cm) loaf pan.

- ■ To give bread a nice glaze, combine egg and 1 tablespoon (15 ml) water; brush top of loaf with mixture.

- ■ Bake for 40 to 45 minutes; brush top with melted butter. Serves 8.

Without question, the greatest invention in the history of mankind is beer. Oh, I grant you that the wheel was also a fine invention, but the wheel does not go nearly as well with pizza.

—Dave Barry

Honey-Oat Bread

2 cups flour	240 g
1¼ cups old-fashioned oats	100 g
1 tablespoon baking powder	15 ml
1 tablespoon brown sugar	15 ml
1 tablespoon honey	15 ml
1 (12 ounce) bottle or can beer	355 ml
¼ cup (½ stick) butter, melted	55 g

■ Preheat oven to 375° (190° C).

■ Combine flour, oats, baking powder, brown sugar and 1 teaspoon (5 ml) salt in large bowl and stir well. Drizzle honey over flour mixture.

■ Pour beer into mixture, a little at a time, and stir after each addition. Stir well to remove most of lumps. Pour batter into sprayed 9 x 5-inch (23 x 13 cm) loaf pan.

■ Bake for 25 to 30 minutes or until golden brown. Brush butter on top and serve hot. Yields 1 loaf.

There can't be good living where there is not good drinking.
—Benjamin Franklin

Onion-Beer Bread

1 cup minced onion	160 g
1 tablespoon butter	15 ml
3 cups flour	360 g
1 tablespoon baking powder	15 ml
1 teaspoon dried oregano	5 ml
1 teaspoon dried thyme	5 ml
2 tablespoons sugar	25 g
1 (12 ounce) bottle or can beer	355 ml
1 egg	
Melted butter	

- ■ Saute onions in butter until translucent, but not brown. Combine flour, baking powder, oregano, thyme and sugar in large bowl; stir in onions.

- ■ Pour beer into mixture, a little at a time, and stir to mix. Pour batter into sprayed 9 x 5-inch (23 x 13 cm) baking pan.

- ■ Beat egg lightly with 1 tablespoon water and brush on top of batter. Let batter rest for about 5 to 10 minutes.

- ■ Preheat oven to 350° (175° C).

- ■ Bake for 45 to 60 minutes. When done, brush top with melted better. Yields 1 loaf.

The word "pub" is short for "public house" first used in England for an establishment that served beer and other alcohol beverages.

Chile-Cheese Bread

1 cup chopped poblano or Anaheim green pepper	120 g
1 cup shredded cheddar cheese	115 g
3 cups flour	360 g
¼ cup sugar	50 g
1 (12 ounce) bottle or can beer	355 ml

■ Preheat oven to 350° (175° C).

■ Process chile pepper and cheese in blender until smooth. Combine flour, sugar and a pinch of salt in large bowl. Add chile-cheese mixture.

■ Slowly pour in beer, a little at a time, and stir after each addition. Pour batter into sprayed 9 x 5-inch (23 x 13 cm) loaf pan.

■ Bake for about 60 minutes or until top is golden brown. Yields 1 loaf.

"Small beer", a very low-alcohol beer, was brewed from the Middle Ages through the 19th century. Because boiling water was a part of the brewing process and there was a small alcohol content, it was substantially safer than the water supply. Small beer was also brewed in households for the children and servants.

Scotchman's Gingerbread

1¾ cups flour	210 g
1¾ cups whole wheat flour	230 g
1 tablespoon ground ginger	15 ml
1 teaspoon ground cinnamon	5 ml
1 teaspoon baking soda	5 ml
¼ teaspoon ground cloves	1 ml
¼ teaspoon ground nutmeg	1 ml
1 cup (2 sticks) butter, softened	225 g
½ cup sugar	100 g
¾ cup molasses	175 ml
2 eggs, slightly beaten	
1 cup beer	250 ml
½ cup raisins	80 g
½ cup diced candied orange peel	65 g
½ cup finely chopped almonds	45 g

■ Preheat oven to 325° (165° C).

■ Combine flour, whole wheat flour, ginger, cinnamon, baking soda, cloves and nutmeg in bowl. In separate large bowl, cream butter, sugar and molasses.

■ Add eggs to butter mixture and beat; add beer slowly and beat. Pour flour mixture, a little at a time, into butter mixture. Add raisins, orange peel and almonds and stir.

■ Pour batter into sprayed and floured 9 x 13-inch (23 x 33 cm) baking pan. Bake for 40 minutes or until golden brown on top. Cool on wire rack. Serves 6 to 8.

Beer Can Bread, Really!

You'll need 8 empty (12 ounce/355 ml) beer cans!

¼ cup (½ stick) butter, softened	55 g
2 eggs, lightly beaten	
1 cup maple syrup	250 ml
1 tablespoon vanilla	15 ml
½ cup golden raisins	75 g
½ cup chopped walnuts	65 g
4 cups whole wheat flour	520 g
2 tablespoons baking soda	30 ml
1⅓ (12 ounce) bottles or cans beer	1⅓ (355 ml)

■ Preheat oven to 350° (175° C).

■ Cream butter, eggs, maple syrup, vanilla, raisins and walnuts in large bowl. Add flour and baking soda, a little at a time, and mix. Pour in beer, a little at a time, and stir well.

■ Remove lids of 8 beer cans and spray inside of cans. Fill each can about halfway with batter and place in a 9 x 13-inch (23 x 33 cm) baking pan.

■ Bake for about 15 minutes or until tops rise, break and are golden brown. Serves 8.

The shelf life of beer is about four months during which time it is at its peak drinkability.

Beer Can Date Bread

This recipe calls for 8 (12 ounce/355 ml) empty beer cans.

2 tablespoons baking soda	30 ml
1 cup chopped dates	150 g
1⅓ (12 ounce) bottles or cans beer	1⅓ (355 ml)
1 cup maple syrup	250 ml
1 tablespoon vanilla	15 ml
3 tablespoons butter	40 g
2 eggs, lightly beaten	
3¾ cups whole wheat flour	490 g
1 cup chopped nuts	170 g

■ You need 8 empty beer cans. Remove tops of cans, rinse and spray inside of each can.

■ Sprinkle baking soda on dates. Heat 1⅓ (12 ounce) bottles or cans of beer to steaming hot, but not boiling. Pour over dates.

■ In separate bowl, cream maple syrup, vanilla, butter and eggs. Stir in flour and nuts. Add dates and beer as soon as they cool.

■ Place empty beer cans with tops removed on large baking sheet and pour batter to about three-quarters of the way in each can.

■ Bake for about 20 minutes. When top splits and toothpick inserted in center comes out clean, date bread is done.

■ Cool and remove bread from cans before serving. Serves 8 to 10.

Tangy Pineapple Bread

1 (8 ounce) can crushed pineapple, drained	225 g
2¾ cups flour	330 g
2 teaspoons baking powder	10 ml
½ cup packed brown sugar	110 g
1 (12 ounce) bottle or can beer	355 ml
½ cup chopped walnuts	65 g
1 cup powdered sugar	120 g
2 tablespoons lemon juice	30 ml

- Preheat oven to 350° (175° C).

- Combine pineapple, flour, baking powder, brown sugar and ½ teaspoon (2 ml) salt in large bowl. Slowly stir in beer and mix lightly just until mixture blends.

- Stir in walnuts and pour into sprayed and floured 9 x 5-inch (23 x 13 cm) loaf pan. Bake for 1 hour or until bread is golden brown on top.

- Cool completely. Combine powdered sugar and lemon juice in bowl and drizzle over top of bread. Yields 1 loaf.

Pilgrims landed at Plymouth Rock instead of the agreed upon Virginia because the ship's stores of beer were low. Sailors on board wanted to return to England with enough beer for the voyage home so they dropped off the Pilgrims earlier than originally planned.

Dizzy Pineapple Bread

1 (8 ounce) can pineapple chunks, drained	225 g
2¾ cups flour	310 g
⅓ cup sugar	65 g
1 (12 ounce) bottle or can beer	355 ml

■ Preheat oven to 350° (175° C).

■ Place pineapple, flour and sugar in large bowl. Slowly pour in beer and stir gently. Pour batter into sprayed 9 x 5-inch (23 x 13 cm) loaf pan.

■ Bake for about 1 hour or until bread is golden brown on top. Yields 1 loaf.

Keep your libraries, your penal institutions, your insane asylums... give me beer. You think man needs rule, he needs beer. The world does not need morals, it needs beer... The souls of men have been fed with indigestibles, but the soul could make use of beer.

—Henry Miller, American novelist

Bacon-Cheddar Beer Bread

3 cups flour	360 g
2 tablespoons sugar	25 g
5 slices bacon, cooked, crumbled	
½ cup shredded cheddar cheese	55 g
1 (12 ounce) bottle or can beer	355 ml

- Preheat oven to 350° (175° C).

- Combine flour, sugar, bacon and cheese in large bowl. Add beer, a little at a time, and stir well. Pour batter into sprayed 9 x 5-inch (23 x 13) loaf pan.

- Bake for about 50 minutes or until bread is golden brown. Cool in loaf pan for a few minutes and turn out onto wire rack. Yields 1 loaf.

The first beer was brewed in the New World by Virginian colonists in 1587 using corn. The first shipment of beer from England arrived in Virginia in 1607. By 1609 a "Help Wanted" sign appeared in London seeking brewers for the Virginia Colony.

Brats-in-a-Blanket

4 cups baking mix	480 g
2 teaspoons caraway seeds	10 ml
1 (12 ounce) can beer	355 ml
2 bratwursts	

- Combine baking mix and caraway seeds in bowl. Slowly pour in beer a little at a time and stir to moisten baking mix. Pour dough about halfway full into 10 sprayed or paper-lined muffin cups.

- Cut brats into 10 pieces and place 1 in each dough-filled muffin cup. Bake for about 18 minutes or until slightly brown on top. Yields 10.

This is grain, which any fool can eat, but for which the Lord intended a more divine means of consumption. Let us give praise to our maker and glory to his bounty by learning about beer.

–Friar Tuck, in Robin Hood, Prince of Thieves

Beer-Cheddar Triangles

2 cups baking mix	240 g
½ cup shredded cheddar cheese	55 g
½ cup beer	125 ml

- ■ Preheat an oven to 450° (230° C).

- ■ Combine baking mix, cheese and beer in bowl and stir until mixture sticks together. Lay wax paper on counter and sprinkle light coating of flour over surface.

- ■ Place batter on floured surface and knead for 2 or 3 minutes. Press dough into 6-inch circle and slice into 10 pie wedges.

- ■ Place wedges on sprayed baking sheet and bake for about 8 minutes or until triangles turn golden brown. Serves 6 to 8.

At the turn of the century in 2000, there were more than 1,500 breweries in the U.S. producing more than 6.2 million barrels of beer with estimated revenue of more than $51 billion.

Beer Cornbread

1 cup yellow cornmeal	160 g
1 cup flour	120 g
¼ cup sugar	50 g
1 tablespoons plus 1 teaspoon baking powder	20 ml
1 (4 ounce) can diced green chilies, drained	115 g
4 green onions with tops, minced	
½ cup shredded cheddar cheese	55 g
½ cup milk	125 ml
½ cup beer	125 ml
1 tablespoon butter, melted	15 ml
1 egg, beaten	

■ Preheat oven to 425° (220° C).

■ Mix cornmeal, flour, sugar, baking powder and ½ teaspoon (2 ml) salt in bowl. Add green chilies, green onions and cheese and mix.

■ Add milk, beer, butter and egg to mixture and stir well. Pour into sprayed 8-inch (20 cm) square baking pan and bake for 20 minutes or until cornbread pulls away from sides of pan and is light brown on top. Serves 4.

24 hours in a day, 24 beers in a case. Coincidence?
—Stephen Wright

Beer-Thyme Biscuits

3 cups flour	360 g
2½ teaspoons baking powder	12 ml
½ teaspoon baking soda	2 ml
1 tablespoon light brown sugar	15 ml
¼ cup fresh thyme leaves	10 g
¼ cup (½ stick) butter, melted	55 g
1 cup cold dark beer	250 ml

■ Preheat oven to 350° (175° C).

■ Combine flour, baking powder, baking soda, brown sugar and thyme in large bowl. Pour in butter and beer and stir until batter forms.

■ Pour batter onto wax paper and knead by hand until batter forms ball. Flatten ball into rectangle about 1-inch (2.5 cm) thick.

■ Divide it into 6 equal portions. Place pieces on baking sheet and bake for about 20 minutes or until biscuits turn golden brown on top. Yields 6.

Flavors are processed in different parts of the tongue. With beer as an example, the slightly bitter flavor of the hops is apparent on the back of the tongue. A salty flavor is experienced on the side of the tongue. And the sweet flavor is experienced on the front of the tongue.

Drunk Biscuits

3¼ cups biscuit mix	390 g
1 teaspoon sugar	5 ml
1⅔ cups beer	400 ml

■ Preheat oven to 400° (205° C).

■ Combine all ingredients and ¼ teaspoon (1 ml) salt in bowl and spoon into 12 sprayed or paper-lined muffin cups.

■ Bake for 15 to 20 minutes or until golden. Serves 8.

Baked French Toast

1 cup milk	250 ml
5 eggs	
½ cup beer	125 ml
¼ cup sugar	50 g
1 teaspoon vanilla	5 ml
8 slices challah or Texas toast	

■ Beat milk, eggs, beer, sugar and vanilla in large bowl with electric mixer on low. Cut each slice of bread into 4 strips and place in sprayed 9 x 13-inch (23 x 33 cm) baking pan.

■ Pour milk mixture over bread and refrigerate overnight.

■ Preheat oven to 425° (205° C). Bake for about 30 minutes or until eggs set and toast is light brown. Serves 4.

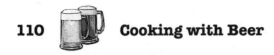

Beer Muffins

3 cups buttermilk baking mix	360 g
¼ cup sugar	50 g
1 cup chopped raisins	160 g
1 cup beer	250 ml

- Preheat oven to 350° (175° C).

- Combine baking mix, sugar, raisins and beer in large bowl and stir well. Pour batter into 10 sprayed or paper-lined muffin cups.

- Bake for about 15 minutes or until golden brown. Yields 10 muffins.

Beer Pancakes

1 cup flour	120 g
¼ cup sugar	50 g
¾ teaspoon baking powder	4 ml
1 egg, beaten	
1 cup beer	250 ml
2 tablespoons butter, melted	30 g

- Combine flour, sugar, baking powder and ½ teaspoon (2 ml) salt in large bowl and stir well. Pour in egg, beer and melted butter and mix until most lumps are gone.

- Heat skillet or griddle to about 350° (175° C). Dip ¼ cup (125 ml) measure into batter, pour onto griddle and repeat for all pancakes. When bubbles come to surface, turn pancakes and cook until brown on both sides. Yields about 10 pancakes.

Crispy Waffles

1 (12 ounce) bottle or can beer	355 ml
½ cup (1 stick) butter, melted	115 g
¼ cup milk	60 ml
2 eggs, separated	
1 tablespoon honey	15 ml
1 teaspoon vanilla	5 ml
2 cups flour	240 g

■ Combine beer, butter, milk, egg yolks, honey and vanilla in large bowl. Add flour, a little at a time, to liquid mixture and stir after each addition. Batter should be smooth.

■ In separate bowl beat egg whites until stiff peaks form. Gently fold egg whites into batter. Spray waffle iron and heat.

■ Pour batter in middle of waffle iron and allow batter to spread before closing lid. Cook waffles until brown and crispy. Serves 4.

The church is near, but the road is icy. The bar is far away, but I will walk carefully.
—Russian proverb

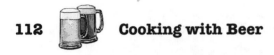

Super Bowl Beer Pretzels

1 cup beer	250 ml
1 tablespoon butter	15 ml
2 tablespoons sugar	25 g
3 cups flour	360 g
¾ teaspoon active dry yeast	4 ml
1 egg, beaten	
2 tablespoons kosher salt	30 g

■ Bread Machine Recipe: Combine beer, butter, sugar, flour, yeast and 1 teaspoon salt in baking pan of bread machine and select Dough/Pasta Setting.

■ Lay wax paper over counter and sprinkle lightly with flour. When cycle is over, remove dough to floured surface. Knead gently until dough is easy to handle.

■ Preheat oven to 350° (175° C).

■ Press into 9 x 13-inch (23 x 33 cm) rectangle and cut into 18 (½-inch/1.2 cm wide) strips. Pull each strip out gently to 16 inches (40 cm) long. Hold both ends and form a circle. Twist ends and place in center of circle.

■ Place on sprayed baking sheet. Add 1 tablespoon warm water to beaten egg and brush over each pretzel. Sprinkle kosher salt over each pretzel and bake for about 18 minutes or until golden brown. Remove from baking sheet to cool. Yields 18 pretzels.

Side Dishes

Backyard Barbecues and Picnics

Backyard barbecues and picnics are enjoyed the world over and many times beer is in the center of the party. Iced down in big ice chests or galvanized tubs, there is nothing quite as good as cold beer in the backyard.

Backyard Barbecues and Picnics

Backyard barbecues and picnics at the park are both great opportunities to get outside and to have some fun. Everything tastes better outside, so light up the grill and cook something great!

Butcher-paper tablecloths with crayons for kids, outdoor games, a big jug of lemonade and tea, ice cold beer and food cooked on the grill is a great way to spend an afternoon or evening. And, don't forget to grab those Frisbees® and, after throwing them all over the yard or park, put your paper plates inside for a sturdy plate holder that can hold lots of food.

Great outdoor games include croquet, badminton, volleyball and bocce. You can wrap them all up with a big finale of water balloons and hide-and-seek. Some of the best foods for those outdoor meals include grilled hot dogs, hamburgers, steaks and kebabs with fruit, vegetables or brats. Try the Rainbow Brat Kebabs (page 205) for a great recipe cooking with beer.

Plan ahead and prepare chickens, turkey, briskets and pork shoulders cooked in a smoker. Tender, juicy meats covered in barbecue sauce or the essence of smoked wood such as mesquite, hickory and pecan can't be beaten.

Everything is livelier, more relaxed, a lot more casual and a lot of fun when you eat outside with the sun or moon overhead and family and friends are all around.

Continued next page...

Continued from previous page...

Have a backyard party or picnic soon and never forget what special memories they create for everyone.

Here are some great backyard favorites.

*Fill with mingled cream and amber;
I will drain that glass again.
Most peculiar visions clamber
through the chambers of my brain.
Quaintest thoughts, queerest fancies,
come to life, and fade away.
What care I how time advances?
I am drinking ale today.*

—Edgar Allan Poe, "Lines on Ale"

Deep-Fried Asparagus

¾ cup flour	90 g
1 teaspoon baking powder	5 ml
½ teaspoon baking soda	2 ml
½ teaspoon celery salt	2 ml
2 egg whites	
⅔ cup cold flat beer	150 ml
2 - 3 pounds fresh asparagus, trimmed	910 g - 1.4 kg
Vegetable oil	

■ Mix flour, baking powder, baking soda, celery salt, and a little salt and pepper. Whisk in egg whites and beer and mix well.

■ Dredge asparagus through batter and carefully drop into hot oil in deep fryer or in large skillet. Fry for about 2 to 3 minutes or until tender and crispy on the outside. Serves 4 to 6.

SAM: What'll you have, Normie?
NORM: Well, I'm in a gambling mood, Sammy. I'll take a glass of whatever comes out of that tap.
SAM: Looks like beer, Norm.
NORM: Call me Mister Lucky.

—Cheers

Broccoli with Ricotta Cheese Sauce

2 bunches green onions with tops	
1 large clove garlic, minced	
Butter	
½ cup plus 2 tablespoons flat amber beer	125 ml/30 ml
1 (1 pound) package ricotta cheese	455 g
¼ cup sour cream	60 g
1 (16 ounce) package frozen broccoli	455 g

■ Mince white part and green tops of green onions separately. Saute white part of green onions and garlic in butter in large saucepan over medium-high heat until onion is translucent.

■ Reduce heat to simmer and add beer, ricotta cheese, sour cream and a little salt and pepper*. Stir and cook until mixture is creamy and hot. (Do not boil.)

■ Prepare broccoli according to package directions. Drain and place in serving bowl. Pour cheese sauce over broccoli and sprinkle minced green onion tops over cheese. Serve immediately. Serves 4.

*TIP: *If you don't like black specks in cheese sauce, use white pepper.*

Because of the carbonation, beer takes up more room than normal ingredients, so be sure to use a big enough bowl.

Beer-Braised Cabbage

½ pound bacon, fried	225 g
2 onions, chopped	
2 cloves garlic, minced	
¼ cup Creole mustard	60 g
1 teaspoon cane syrup or honey	5 ml
1 (12 ounce) bottle dark beer	355 ml
1 head cabbage, chopped	
¼ cup whipping cream	60 ml

- In large saucepan or skillet, fry bacon and drain all but 2 to 3 tablespoons (30 to 45 ml) drippings. Saute onion and garlic in drippings until translucent.

- Reduce heat to medium and add mustard, syrup and beer. Add cabbage, a little at a time, and coat cabbage. Cover and cook for about 15 minutes.

- Add cream and a little salt and pepper, stir well and cook for additional 5 to 10 minutes or until dish is warm. Serves 4 to 6.

Do you know the origin of the term "whet your whistle"? Would you believe that several centuries ago, pub clientele ordered their brews by whistling. They even had whistles molded into ceramic mugs to make it as easy as possible to get the proprietor's attention.

Beer-Steamed Sauerkraut

1 (16 ounce) jar sauerkraut	455 g
1 (12 ounce) bottle or can beer	355 ml
2 tablespoons sugar	25 g
1 - 2 teaspoons chili powder	5 - 10 ml

- Place sauerkraut and beer in saucepan over medium heat and cook for 20 minutes. (Do not boil.)

- Add sugar and chili powder and cook until liquid reduces by half. Drain and serve immediately. Serves 4.

Smokin' Corn-on-the-Cob

12 ears fresh corn-on-the-cob with husks	
2 quarts light beer	2 L
1 (10 pound) bag ice	4.5 kg

- Peel husks back three-fourths down the cob, but do not remove. Pull off as many silks as possible and wrap husks around corn. Place in cooler and pour beer over corn. Open ice bag and pour into cooler, close cooler and marinate corn for 5 or 6 hours.

- When ready to cook corn, heat grill. Drain corn and place on rack in grill over medium heat and close lid. Corn is cooked when kernels are tender. Peel back husks and use as handles. Serves 8 to 10.

Southern Dixie Greens

½ pound sliced bacon	225 g
1 large onion, chopped	
4 green onions with tops, chopped	
Cayenne pepper	
1 (12 ounce) bottle Dixie beer	355 ml
¼ cup rice wine vinegar	60 ml
1 tablespoon molasses	15 ml
4 - 5 pounds mustard greens, collard greens, turnip greens or kale, stemmed	1.8 - 2.3 kg

■ Fry bacon in large roasting pan until crispy. Drain bacon and set aside. Saute onion and green onions in bacon drippings until translucent. Season with a little salt, pepper and cayenne pepper.

■ Pour in beer, wine vinegar and molasses and stir well. Cook over medium-high heat, but do not boil. Add greens, a little at a time, and stir to coat greens with liquid.

■ Cook greens uncovered for about 1 hour or until greens are tender. Serves 6 to 8.

Did you know that there are different percentages of alcohol in various beers? In the United States the range is from 3.2% to 8% alcohol. The alcohol content of European beers ranges from less than 3% to 13%.

Southern Collard Greens

1 pound collard greens, stemmed	455 g
1 (12 ounce) bottle or can beer	355 ml
½ pound sliced bacon, cut into pieces	225 g
¼ teaspoon sugar	1 ml

■ Wash greens well and break into pieces. Combine beer, 2 cups (500 ml) water, 1 teaspoon (5 ml) salt and bacon in large roasting pan or soup pot. Add greens and stir well.

■ Cook greens on medium-high until leaves wilt, about 5 to 10 minutes. Reduce heat to low, cover and cook for about 1 hour 30 minutes. Serves 4.

Southern-Style Onion Rings

1 (12 ounce) bottle or can light beer	355 ml
2 cups flour	240 g
3 - 4 large Texas 1015 SuperSweet or Vidalia®	
sweet onions, sliced, separated into rings	
Oil	

■ Pour beer, a little at a time, into flour mixed with a little salt and stir after each addition. Coat onions with batter.

■ Carefully place onion rings in hot oil in large skillet. Fry until golden brown and drain on paper towel. Serve immediately. Serves 4 to 6.

Scotch Ale Potatoes

1 (12 ounce) bottle Scotch Ale	355 ml
4 green onions with tops, chopped	
¼ cup crushed rosemary	10 g
1 teaspoon garlic salt	5 ml
10 - 12 small new potatoes with peel, sliced	
2 medium onions, chopped	
Grated parmesan cheese	

- ■ Combine ale, green onions, rosemary and garlic salt in large resealable plastic bag. Add potatoes and onions and marinate for 1 to 2 hours.

- ■ Preheat oven to 375° (190° C).

- ■ Use slotted spoon to remove potatoes and onions from marinade. Place in baking dish and pour about ½ cup (125 ml) marinade over vegetables.

- ■ Cover dish and bake for 30 minutes. Remove from oven and stir. Season with a little salt and pepper.

- ■ Sprinkle parmesan cheese over potatoes and bake uncovered for additional 10 to 15 minutes. Serves 6 to 8.

Carbonation happens when carbon dioxide is injected into a beverage or is created in the fermenting process.

Redneck
Fried Green Tomatoes

1½ cups flour	180 g
1 teaspoon garlic powder	5 ml
½ teaspoon cayenne pepper	2 ml
2 eggs, lightly beaten	
1 (12 fluid ounce) can beer	355 ml
4 large green tomatoes, thickly sliced	
Oil	

■ Mix flour, garlic powder and cayenne pepper. Stir in eggs; then slowly pour beer into mixture, a little at a time, and stir after each addition. Consistency will be thick batter, like pancake batter.

■ Dredge tomato slices through batter and coat both sides. Carefully place in hot oil and fry until golden brown on both sides. Serves 6 to 8.

I feel sorry for people who don't drink. When they wake up in the morning, that's as good as they're going to feel all day.
—Frank Sinatra

Not Some Stuffy Tomatoes

6 - 8 large, ripe tomatoes
3 cups soft breadcrumbs   175 g
1 (11 ounce) can whole kernel corn, drained   310 g
1 (8 ounce) package shredded cheddar cheese 225 g
1 medium onion, minced
1 (12 ounce) bottle stout   355 ml

■   Preheat oven to 350° (175° C).

■   Remove tops of tomatoes, scoop out flesh and drain. (Do
     not discard flesh.) Mix breadcrumbs, corn, cheese and
     onion. Sprinkle a little salt and pepper in mixture. Stir in
     drained tomato flesh.

■   Place several scoops of stuffing in each tomato. Place
     stuffed tomatoes in baking dish and pour stout over
     tomatoes. Bake for about 20 minutes or until tops brown.
     Serves 6 to 8.

*Did you know that beer helped Louis Pasteur
develop the pasteurization process for milk?
Much of his research for the pasteurization
process was done on beer and one of his most
famous treatises is "Studies Concerning Beer".
What he learned from beer helped him to develop
the process by which today many of our beverages
are made safer.*

Boston's Best:
Beer and Beans

2 pounds dry navy beans	910 g
2 (12 ounce) bottles Samuel Adams Boston Lager®, divided	2 (355 ml)
1 (1 pound) package bacon slices	455 g
2 large onions, chopped	
1¾ cups packed brown sugar	385 g
⅓ cup prepared mustard	85 g

■ Soak beans in water overnight. Drain, cover beans with water and 1 (12 ounce/355 ml) bottle beer. Place several slices of bacon in beans for seasoning.

■ Cook over medium-high heat, but do not boil. Reduce heat and cook on low for 1 hour or until beans are tender.

■ Preheat oven to 300° (150° C).

■ Season with brown sugar, mustard and a little salt and pepper. Pour beans and liquid into 9 x 13-inch (23 x 33 cm) baking dish.

■ Place remaining bacon on top of beans in rows. Add enough of remaining beer to cover beans. Bake uncovered for about 2 hours 30 minutes. Serves 8.

Beer Beans

1 pound dried pinto beans, washed	455 g
2 (14 ounce) cans chicken broth	2 (395 g)
1 (12 ounce) bottle or can dark beer	355 ml
2 (14 ounce) cans chopped stewed tomatoes	2 (395 g)
1½ cups chopped fresh cilantro	25 g
1 large onion, minced	
¼ cup chopped pickled jalapenos	30 g
6 cloves garlic, minced	

■ Cover beans with water and soak overnight. Drain and pour in chicken broth and beer. (Beans should be covered with liquid. Add water if you don't have enough broth and beer.)

■ Cover pot and bring almost to boil, but do not boil. Add tomatoes, cilantro, onion, jalapenos and garlic. Reduce heat to medium low and continue cooking for about 4 hours.

■ Keep plenty of liquid in pot and stir occasionally. When beans are tender, use potato masher to mash about 1 cup (250 ml) beans to thicken liquid. Season with salt and pepper to taste. Serves 6 to 8.

TIP: After serving beans, mash leftovers to make bean dip and serve with chips.

Frijoles Borrachos

(Drunken Beans)

1 (16 ounce) package dry pinto beans	455 g
1 (12 ounce) can dark Mexican beer	355 ml
4 - 6 jalapenos, stemmed, seeded, minced*	
1 onion, chopped	
2 tomatoes, chopped	
2 teaspoons Worcestershire sauce	10 ml

■ Sort pinto beans, rinse and soak in water overnight.
When ready to cook, drain beans and pour in beer and
enough water to cover.

■ Cook on medium-high, but do not boil and cook on low
for 2 to 3 hours or until beans are almost tender. (Add
water if necessary.)

■ Drain 2 cups (500 ml) liquid from pot and set aside.
If remaining juice is too thin, add enough dry potato
flakes to thicken. Add jalapenos, onion, tomatoes and
Worcestershire.

■ Simmer for 30 minutes to blend flavors and serve.
Taste and add salt, if needed, in the last few minutes
of cooking. Serves 8.

TIP: Wear rubber gloves to handle jalapenos.

Pecos Whistleberries

3 cups dry pinto beans, washed	430 g
2 tablespoons chili powder	15 g
1 jalapeno pepper, seeded, sliced*	
¼ cup chopped onion	40 g
2 teaspoons garlic powder	10 ml
½ teaspoon ground cumin	2 ml
2 tablespoons cilantro	30 ml
3 tablespoons ketchup	50 g
¼ cup (½ stick) butter	55 g
1 (12 ounce) bottle or can beer	355 ml
Flour tortillas and jalapenos	

■ Place beans in 8-quart (8 L) saucepan, pour 5 quarts (5 L) boiling water over beans and soak overnight.

■ Drain water and add just enough fresh water to cover beans. Cook on high for 30 minutes. Lower heat and add remaining ingredients. (Do not boil.) Add more beer if needed.

■ Cover and simmer for 2 hours 30 minutes to 3 hours or until beans are soft. Add 1 teaspoon (5 ml) salt before serving. Serve hot with flour tortillas and jalapenos. Serves 14 to 16.

*TIP: Wear rubber gloves when handling jalapenos.

Firecracker Pinto Beans

1 (1 pound) bag dry pinto beans	455 g
1 (12 ounce) bottle dark beer	355 ml
1 large onion, chopped	
½ pound sliced bacon, cut in pieces	225 g
4 cloves garlic, minced	
1 fresh jalapeno, seeded, minced*	
1 (4 ounce) can diced chipotle chilies	115 g
Shredded cheddar cheese	

■ Cover beans with water and soak overnight. Drain, rinse beans and cover with water to about 1 inch (2.5 cm) above beans in large soup pot. Pour in beer.

■ Add onion, bacon, garlic, jalapeno and chipotle chilies. Cook, uncovered, on low to medium heat for 2 to 3 hours or until beans are tender. Do not boil. Add more water, if necessary.

■ Season with salt to taste and serve with cheese. Serves 6 to 8.

TIP: Wear rubber gloves when handling jalapenos.

*I would give all my fame
for a pot of ale and safety.*
—Shakespeare, Henry V

Trail Drive Whistlers

2 pounds dried pinto beans	910 g
1 medium piece salt pork	
5 slices bacon, chopped	
2 (10 ounce) cans diced tomatoes and	
green chilies	2 (280 g)
1 onion, chopped	
1 (12 ounce) bottle or can beer	355 ml
¼ teaspoon oregano	1 ml
½ teaspoon ground cumin	2 ml
2 teaspoons minced garlic	10 ml

■ Rinse pinto beans and place in large saucepan. Cover with water and soak overnight or for at least 3 hours. Drain and add just enough water to cover beans.

■ Add salt pork, bacon, tomatoes and green chilies, and onion to soup pot. Bring to a boil, lower heat and add beer. Simmer for 3 hours or until beans are tender. Add beer or water if more liquid is needed.

■ Add oregano, cumin, garlic and ½ teaspoon (2 ml) salt in the last 30 minutes of cooking. Serves 10 to 14.

The aluminum can was introduced by Coors of Golden, Colorado in 1959. The tab top was introduced by Pittsburgh Brewing Company in 1962. The ring-pull tab was introduced in 1965.

Vegetarian Favorite Pasta

¾ cup diced onion	120 g
2 cloves garlic, minced	
1 (8 ounce) carton button mushrooms	225 g
¼ cup olive oil	60 ml
1 (28 ounce) can stewed tomatoes	795 g
1 cup pale ale	250 ml
1 (6 ounce) can tomato paste	170 g
1 teaspoon minced fresh basil	5 ml
1 teaspoon dried oregano	5 ml
1 (8 ounce) package your favorite pasta	225 g

■ Place onion, garlic and mushrooms in large saucepan and saute in a little oil over medium-high heat until onion is translucent.

■ Add stewed tomatoes, pale ale, tomato paste, basil and oregano and stir well. Reduce heat to medium-low and cook for about 30 minutes. (Do not boil.) Stir several times and taste for seasonings.

■ Add beer or water if sauce gets too thick. Simmer covered for 5 more minutes. Prepare pasta according to package directions, drain and serve with sauce. Serves 4.

Life, alas, is very drear. Up with the glass! Down with the beer!
–Louis Untermeyer

Beer-Pickled Eggs

12 eggs, hard-boiled, shelled
½ (12 ounce) bottle or can beer   ½ (355 ml)
1 cup vinegar   250 ml
2 tablespoons parsley flakes   30 ml
2 teaspoons pickling spice   10 ml

- Prick eggs in several places with toothpick so liquid can permeate egg white. Place eggs in glass jars.

- Mix beer, vinegar, parsley flakes and pickling spice in pitcher. Pour over eggs and cover completely.

- Place lids on jars and refrigerate for at least 3 days before serving. Good for 2 weeks in refrigerator. Serves 10 to 12.

According to the Oklahoma Malt Beverage Association "breathalyzers work on a clever electrochemical principle. The subject's breath is passed over a platinum electrode which causes the alcohol to bind with oxygen, forming acetic acid. In the process it loses two electrons, a process that sets up a current in a wire connected to the electrode. The higher the concentration of alcohol in the breath, the greater the electrical current, which can be read by a simple meter to indicate intoxication levels." www.oklahomabeer.org

Main Dishes

Beef, Chicken, Pork & Seafood

St. Patrick's Day

St. Patrick's Day, Ireland and beer are synonymous with and symbolic of the popular celebration memorializing the patron saint of Ireland. For more than 1,600 years beer has been at the center of St. Patrick's Day as it is celebrated around the world.

St. Patrick's Day

A religious feast was first held on March 17 in the 5th century to celebrate the anniversary of the death of St. Patrick, the patron saint of Ireland. Today, Irish descendents and "want-to-be" Irishmen celebrate this same holiday that has become one of the most popular worldwide holidays.

The celebration began in the New World as soon as an Irishman set foot on land. Each year the celebration grew and on March 17, 1762 New York City celebrated the holiday with a parade.

Today the New York City St. Patrick's Day Parade is the world's oldest civilian parade and has more than 150,000 participants. Other cities all over the world host parades with bagpipes, drums and green beer in abundance and there's no mistaking centuries of Irish pride.

Dublin is the site of the largest St. Patrick's Day celebration with more than 1,000,000 people participating in the event.

It wasn't until the mid-1990's that the Irish government began marketing St. Patrick's Day to promote tourism, but the holiday was well established by the Irish people long before.

For hundreds of years, pubs were closed in Ireland for the holiday, but beer flowed freely in every home. It was considered a staple in households and helped prolong life because it cut down on drinking contaminated water.

The shamrock was recognized as a symbol of the Holy Trinity as early as the 17th century and the "wearing of the green" became an early tradition. Wearing green on one's clothing is now the only way to avoid being pinched by an Irishman, which is tricky because on St. Paddy's Day everyone is an Irishman.

Continued next page...

Continued from previous page...

The tradition of the "green" has taken on many forms since the 17th century and one of the most notable is when the City of Chicago dyes the Chicago River green on St. Patrick's Day.

In 1962 Chicago pollution-control workers used a green dye to trace illegal pollution. It turned out to be such an interesting feature that the practice became a tradition and on every St. Patrick's Day the City of Chicago wears its green on its river.

Traditional foods for the day include Traditional Irish Stew (page 161) Irish Corned Beef and Cabbage (page 157), but the most authentic is bacon and cabbage or ham and cabbage. Corned beef and cabbage is an Americanized version of the Irish tradition.

Irish toasts are usually at the center of every pub or party and here are some that you may remember at your next St. Patrick's Day party.

- *Thirst is a shameless disease, so here's to a shameful cure.*

- *Here's to a wet night and a dry morning.*

- *Morning is the time to pity the sober. The way they're feeling then is the best they'll feel all day.*

With a little luck from the Irish, try these special dishes for any occasion.

Spicy Meatballs and Spaghetti

2 (19 ounce) bottles hot and spicy ketchup	2 (540 g)
2 (12 ounce) bottles or cans beer	2 (355 ml)
2 pounds ground round	910 g
2 cloves garlic, minced	
1 onion, minced	
½ cup cooked rice	80 g
Vegetable oil	
Spaghetti	

■ Turn slow cooker to HIGH and pour in ketchup and beer. Cover and cook for about 30 minutes or until mixture begins to steam, but do not boil.

■ Combine beef, garlic, onion and cooked rice in large bowl. Shape mixture into small balls and place in hot oil in skillet. Brown on all sides, drain on paper towels and place in slow cooker.

■ Cover and cook on LOW for about 3 hours. Prepare spaghetti according to package directions. Serve meatballs and sauce over spaghetti or serve without spaghetti as hors d'oeuvres. Serves 4.

 There are over 200 styles of beer produced throughout the world.

Simple No-Patty Sandwiches

1 (pound) package ground beef	455 g
1 (12 ounce) bottle or can beer	355 ml
2 teaspoons prepared yellow mustard	10 ml
1 teaspoon sugar	5 ml
Hamburger buns	

■ Brown ground beef in skillet over medium-high heat until all pink is gone. Drain grease and discard.

■ Pour beer into skillet. Mix mustard, sugar, ½ teaspoon (2 ml) salt and ½ teaspoon (2 ml) pepper and combine with ground beef. Bring almost to boil, reduce heat and cook on low until liquid reduces. Serve on hamburger buns. Serves 3 to 4.

Always remember that I have taken more out of alcohol than alcohol has taken out of me.
—Winston Churchill

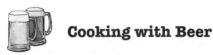

Sunday Roast/ Monday Night Sandwiches

8 potatoes, peeled, quartered	
4 carrots, sliced	
2 onions, quartered	
1 (3 pound) rump roast	1.4 kg
1 (12 ounce) bottle or can beer	355 ml
1 (14 ounce) can beef broth	395 g
1 (10 ounce) can French onion soup	280 g
French rolls	
Butter	

■ Place potatoes, carrots and onions in bottom of sprayed slow cooker. Position roast on top of vegetables and sprinkle with salt and pepper.

■ Pour beer, beef broth and French onion soup over roast. Cover and cook on LOW for 7 to 8 hours or on HIGH for 4 hours or until tender.

Sunday Roast:

■ Serve for big weekend meal and save leftovers and sauce for weeknight.

Monday Night:

■ Slice French rolls horizontally and spread with butter. Bake in oven at 350° (175° C) for about 10 minutes.

■ Cut leftover roast into very thin slices and place on French rolls. Serve with sauce in slow cooker for dipping. Serves 4 plus leftovers.

Mushroom-Covered Roast Beef

1 (1 pound) carton sliced fresh mushrooms, stemmed	455 g
1 (2 - 3 pound) chuck roast	910 g - 1.4 kg
1 (12 ounce) bottle beer	355 ml
1 (1 ounce) packet onion soup mix	30 g

■ Place mushrooms in bottom of sprayed slow cooker and place roast on top. Pour beer into slow cooker and sprinkle soup mix on top.

■ Cover and cook on LOW for 8 to 9 hours or until meat falls apart. Serves 4 to 5.

A good local pub has much in common with a church, except that a pub is warmer and there's more conversation.

—William Blake

Family Affair Roast

1 (3 pound) beef rump roast	1.4 kg
1 (14 ounce) can beef broth	395 g
1 (10 ounce) can French onion soup	280 g
1 (12 ounce) bottle or can beer	355 ml
4 potatoes, quartered	
3 onions, quartered	
1 (16 ounce) package baby carrots	455 g

- Season rump roast with a little salt and pepper and place in sprayed slow cooker. Pour broth, soup and beer over roast, cover and cook on LOW for about 6 hours.

- Remove roast and place potatoes, onions and carrots in bottom of slow cooker. Place roast on top of vegetables. Continue cooking covered for additional 2 hours. Serves 8.

Before many battles, the Vikings drank a bucket or two of ale. When they were ready, they ripped off their shirts and ran madly into battle. The Norse word "berserk" meant "bare shirt"; thus, the extended version of the word means "running wildly into battle without a shirt".

Roasted Chuck

1 (3 - 4 pound) chuck roast	1.4 - 1.8 kg
1 cup barbecue sauce	265 g
1 cup teriyaki sauce	250 ml
1 (12 ounce) bottle or can beer	355 ml
4 cloves garlic, minced	
1 tablespoon thinly sliced fresh ginger root	15 ml
3 onions, chopped	

- ■ Mix barbecue sauce, teriyaki sauce, beer, garlic, ginger, onions, and 2 teaspoons (10 ml) each of pepper and salt in bowl. Place roast in roasting pan, pour marinade over roast and cover pan with plastic wrap. Marinate in refrigerator for about 4 hours; turn frequently to cover meat.

- ■ When ready to bake, allow roasting pan to reach room temperature and preheat oven to 350° (175° C). Bake for 3 to 4 hours or until tender.

- ■ Add water or beer if more liquid is needed. Serves 8 to 10.

If God had intended us to drink beer,
He would have given us stomachs.
—David Daye

Beef, Beer and Onions

2 pounds chuck or round beef roast	910 g
2 tablespoons butter	30 g
2 tablespoons oil	30 ml
5 - 6 medium onions, peeled, sliced	
1½ tablespoons flour	22 ml
2 cups dark beer	500 ml
2 - 3 sprigs fresh thyme	
1 bay leaf, crumpled	
Cooked noodles or rice	

■ Preheat oven to 350° (175° C).

■ Sprinkle both sides of roast generously with salt and pepper. Add butter and olive oil to large roasting pan and brown meat on both sides over medium-high heat quickly. Remove beef.

■ Add sliced onions to drippings. Reduce heat and cook onions until translucent; stir often. Add flour to onions. Cook, stirring constantly, until flour is light brown.

■ Add beer to flour and stir until mixture thickens. Add thyme and bay leaf. Return beef to pan and cover.

■ Bake for about 2 hours or until meat is tender. Check liquid around beef; add more beer or water if necessary.

■ Slice into several pieces and serve over buttered noodles or rice. Serves 6 to 8.

Do-Re-Me Steak Fingers

1 (1 - 2 pound) venison roast	455 - 910 g
1 (12 ounce) bottle or can beer	355 ml
½ cup Worcestershire sauce	125 ml
1 cup flour	120 g
2 teaspoons onion salt	10 ml
2 teaspoons garlic powder	10 ml
Oil	

■ Carve venison into 6 x 2 x ⅜-inch (15 x 5 x 1 cm) thick slices and tenderize. Place in sprayed baking dish. Pour beer and Worcestershire over venison, cover with plastic wrap and refrigerate for about 1 hour.

■ In separate dish, mix flour, onion salt, garlic powder and ½ teaspoon (2 ml) pepper. Dredge venison strips through flour and coat all sides. Discard marinade.

■ Place venison in large skillet with a little hot oil and fry on medium low until juices run clear. Serves 6.

Prohibition makes you want to cry into your beer and denies you the beer to cry into.
—Don Marquis

Beer-Braised Brisket

4 slices bacon	
1 (2½ pound) beef brisket, trimmed	1.1 kg
3 onions, sliced thin	
4 cloves garlic, peeled, sliced	
4 (12 ounce) bottles lager	4 (355 ml)
12 fingerling potatoes with peel	
4 carrots, peeled, sliced	
1 bay leaf, broken in half	
¼ cup (½ stick) butter, softened	55 g
3 tablespoons flour	25 g

- ■ Preheat oven to 350° (175° C).

- ■ Cook bacon in large roasting pan over medium-high heat until crisp. Drain on paper towels; when cool crumble into bits. Save 2 tablespoons (30 ml) bacon drippings from pan and discard remaining grease.

- ■ Season brisket with salt and pepper on both sides. Brown brisket on both sides in bacon drippings to seal in juices. Remove brisket from pan and set aside.

- ■ Add onion and garlic and cook until translucent. Pour beer into roasting pan and cook several minutes over medium heat; scrape brown bits off bottom and sides of pan.

- ■ Add brisket and bacon bits to roasting pan, cover and bake for 2 hours.

- ■ Add potatoes, carrots and bay leaf to brisket. Spoon pan juices over brisket and vegetables. Cover and cook additional 30 to 45 minutes or until brisket falls apart.

Continued next page...

Continued from previous page...

■ Place brisket on large ovenproof platter with vegetables; discard bay leaf. Reduce heat to 200° (95° C) and place in oven to keep warm.

■ Combine butter and flour until creamy. Add to hot pan juices and cook over medium heat on stovetop. Whisk for several minutes until it thickens. Adjust seasonings.

■ When brisket cools a little, slice thinly across grain. Serve with gravy over top and on the side. Serves 6 to 8.

But if at church they would give some ale. And a pleasant fire our souls to regale. We'd sing and we'd pray all the live long day, nor ever once from the church to stray.

–William Blake

Slow-Cooked Brisket

3 cloves garlic, minced	
10 pounds untrimmed beef brisket	4.5 kg
1 (12 ounce) can beer	355 ml
2 (18 ounce) bottles hickory smoke-flavored	
barbecue sauce	2 (510 g)
1 cup molasses	250 ml
2 tablespoons liquid smoke	30 ml
2 large onions, sliced	

■ Sprinkle garlic and 1 tablespoon (15 ml) each of salt and pepper over brisket and place in large roasting pan.

■ Mix beer, barbecue sauce, molasses and liquid smoke and pour over brisket. Place onions around brisket.

■ Cover and cook in oven at 300° (150° C) for about 6 hours or until beef is tender. Let stand about 10 to 15 minutes before trimming fat and thinly slicing brisket across grain. Serves 8 to 10.

After 300 years of continuous operation of breweries in Boston, the last Boston brewery closed in 1964. In 1984, the Boston Beer Company was founded and continues the Boston brewing tradition, producing Samuel Adams Lager and other beers.

Beef Medallions in Beer Sauce

4 (6 - 8 ounce) beef medallions	4 (170 - 225 g)
Butter	
6 - 8 green onions with tops, minced	
2 cloves garlic, minced	
1 (8 ounce) carton fresh button mushrooms, sliced	225 g
1 cup diced tomatoes	180 g
1 (14 ounce) can beef broth	395 g
1 (12 ounce) bottle or can beer, divided	355 ml
1 - 2 tablespoons flour	15 - 30 ml

- Sear medallions on both sides in large skillet in butter over medium to high heat to seal in juices.

- Reduce heat to medium-low and add green onions, garlic, mushrooms, tomatoes, broth and half the beer.

- Cook uncovered over medium heat to desired temperature. Remove medallions, add flour and a little salt and pepper and stir well to make sauce. (Add beer if more liquid is needed.)

- Stir continuously to thicken. Serve over medallions. Serves 4.

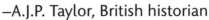

In my opinion, most of the great men of the past were only there for the beer.

–A.J.P. Taylor, British historian

Old El Paso Fajitas

El Paso claims to be the home of the first fajitas.

1 (1 pound) skirt steak	455 g
1 (12 ounce) bottle or can beer	355 ml
⅓ cup freshly squeezed lime juice	75 ml
3 onions, sliced	
1 green bell pepper, seeded, thick sliced	
1 red bell pepper, seeded, thick sliced	
1 teaspoon garlic salt	5 ml
1 teaspoon lemon pepper	5 ml
1 teaspoon onion powder	5 ml
Flour tortillas	
Sour cream, shredded cheese,	
guacamole, pico de gallo	

■ Tenderize skirt steak to about ¼-inch (6 mm) thick and place in glass baking dish. Mix beer, lime juice, onions and bell peppers and pour over steaks.

■ Cover with plastic wrap and refrigerate for about 2 hours. Turn several times while marinating.

■ Remove steaks and discard marinade liquid, keeping onions and bell peppers. Sprinkle both sides of steak with garlic salt, lemon pepper and onion powder.

■ Cook steak, onions and bell peppers on grill over medium heat until done. Slice steak across grain into thin strips. Serve with flour tortillas, sour cream, shredded cheese, guacamole and pico de gallo as desired. Serves 4.

Gingered Flank Steak

1 (12 ounce) bottle or can beer, flat	355 ml
½ cup olive oil	125 ml
¼ cup orange zest	25 g
2 tablespoons minced fresh ginger	30 ml
2 cloves garlic, minced	
1 (1½ - 2 pound) flank steak	(680 - 910 g)

■ Combine all ingredients except steak in glass dish. Sprinkle a little salt and pepper over steak and place in marinade. Marinate in refrigerator for 12 to 24 hours and turn several times. Discard marinade.

■ Cook steak slowly on grill over low heat to desired doneness. Slice very thinly across grain. Serves 4.

Beer will always have a definite role in the diet of an individual and can be considered a cog in the wheel of nutritional foods.
—Bruce Carlton

Grilled Flat-Iron Steak

1 (1½ pound) flat-iron steak	680 g
½ cup beer	125 ml
¼ cup teriyaki sauce	60 ml
¼ cup packed brown sugar	55 g
1 tablespoon cracked black pepper	15 ml
1 red bell pepper, seeded, sliced	
1 green bell pepper, seeded, sliced	
6 - 8 small onions	
¼ cup extra-virgin olive oil	60 ml
2 tablespoons balsamic vinegar	30 ml
4 medium tomatoes	

■ Season flat-iron steak with a little salt and pepper and place in baking dish. Mix beer, teriyaki sauce, brown sugar and cracked black pepper in bowl. Pour over steak, cover with plastic wrap and refrigerate for about 1 hour. Turn frequently.

■ Place bell peppers and onions in bowl. Mix olive oil and vinegar and pour over vegetables.

■ Place steak on grill over low fire and cook slowly until medium rare. (Cooking too fast and too well done will make steak tough.)

■ Add bell pepper and onions next to steak and cook until grill marks appear on both sides. Place vegetables on top of steak to keep warm.

■ About 5 minutes before taking steak off grill, place tomatoes on grill to cook. Remove when tender.

■ Thinly slice steak at an angle. Serve meat with vegetables on top. Serves 4 to 6.

Marinated Brown Beer Steaks

¼ cup dark beer	60 ml
¼ cup teriyaki sauce	60 ml
2 tablespoons brown sugar	30 g
½ teaspoon seasoned salt	2 ml
½ teaspoon garlic powder	2 ml
2 (16 ounce) sirloin steaks	2 (455 g)

■ Mix beer, teriyaki sauce and brown sugar in bowl. Place steaks in flat dish and sprinkle with a little salt and pepper on both sides. Pour beer mixture over steaks and marinate at room temperature for about 10 minutes.

■ Discard marinade. Season steaks with seasoned salt, garlic powder and pepper and let rest for about 10 minutes. Place steaks on grill over medium-hot fire and sear both sides. Reduce heat to medium-low and cook for desired flavor. Serves 4.

*I believe this would be
a good time for a beer.*
—Franklin D. Roosevelt
on signing the 21st amendment
(repeal of Prohibition)

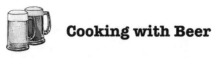

Marinated Rib-Eye Steaks

4 (6 - 8 ounce) rib-eye steaks   4 (170 - 225 g)
2 (12 ounce) bottles or cans beer   2 (355 ml)
Seasoned salt
Lemon pepper

- ■ Place steaks in baking dish and pour beer over top. Marinate in refrigerator, covered with plastic wrap, for about 3 hours and turn several times.

- ■ Discard beer, sprinkle steaks with seasoned salt and lemon pepper and grill over medium fire for about 3 to 5 minutes per side. Serves 4.

Beer should be as fresh as possible to enjoy the mix of flavors. The lighter the beer, the colder it should be. The best temperature for light beer such as Pilsner and lager is 45° (7° C). The best temperature for stronger beers such as ales is 55° (13° C) because the flavors are more complex.

Sam Adams' Favorite Sirloin

1 (2 - 3 pound) sirloin steak	910 g - 1.4 kg
2 (12 ounce) bottles Samuel Adams	
Boston Lager®	2 (355 ml)
2 teaspoons canola oil	10 ml
2 cloves garlic, minced	
1 tablespoon lemon pepper	15 ml
1 teaspoon seasoned salt	5 ml

■ Place steak in glass baking dish and pour enough beer over steak to cover. Marinate in refrigerator for 2 to 3 hours.

■ Remove steak, pat dry and rub oil on both sides of steak. Discard marinade. Sprinkle garlic, lemon pepper and seasoned salt on both sides of steak and rub in.

■ Place steak on grill over medium-hot fire and sear both sides. Reduce heat and cook over medium-low heat until center is medium rare.

■ Remove from grill and slice into 4 serving-size pieces. Serve immediately. Serves 4.

[I recommend]... *bread, meat, vegetables and beer.*
—Sophocles' philosophy of a moderate diet

Slow-Cooker Steak Bites

1 (2½ - 3 pounds) round steak	1.1 - 1.4 kg
1 (1 ounce) packet brown gravy mix	30 g
1 (1 ounce) packet onion soup mix	30 g
⅓ cup flour	40 g
1 (14 ounce) can beef broth	395 g
1 (12 ounce) bottle or can beer	355 ml

- Cut round steak into bite-size pieces, place in sprayed slow cooker and sprinkle with a little salt and pepper.

- Mix brown gravy mix, onion soup mix and flour in small bowl. Sprinkle over round steak and stir. Pour broth and beer into slow cooker and cover.

- Cook on LOW for about 6 to 8 hours. Serves 8.

The Pilgrims planned their first Thanksgiving for Virginia, but landed in Plymouth Rock instead and celebrated their first Thanksgiving there. Would you believe they were running out of food, water and "especially our beere", as one of the Pilgrims wrote?

Slow-Cooker
Steak and Potatoes

4 - 6 potatoes, peeled, sliced	
1 large onion, sliced	
1 (2 pounds) round steak	910 g
1 tablespoon brown sugar	15 ml
¼ teaspoon ground nutmeg	1 ml
¼ teaspoon cracked black pepper	1 ml
1 (1 ounce) package beef-onion soup mix	30 g
1 (12 ounce) bottle or can beer	355 ml

■ Place potatoes and onions in bottom of sprayed slow cooker. Cut round steak in serving-size pieces and position on top of vegetables.

■ Sprinkle brown sugar, 1 teaspoon salt, nutmeg, cracked black pepper and onion soup mix over steak. Pour beer into slow cooker.

■ Cover and cook on LOW for 6 to 8 hours or until beef is fork tender. Serves 6 to 8.

May your glass be ever full. May the roof over your head be always strong. And may you be in heaven half an hour before the devil knows you're dead.

—Old Irish Toast

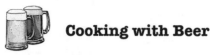

Beered-Up Jerky

1 (1 pound) round steak	455 g
½ (12 ounce) bottle beer	½ (355 ml)
¾ cup teriyaki sauce	175 ml
½ cup Worcestershire sauce	125 ml
⅓ cup soy sauce	75 ml
¼ cup liquid smoke	60 ml
2 tablespoons ketchup	35 g
1 teaspoon cracked black pepper	5 ml
½ teaspoon garlic powder	2 ml

- Tenderize round steak. Cut into strips about 1-inch (2.5 cm) wide, about 5 inches (13 cm) long and about ¼-inch (6 mm) thick.

- Mix beer, teriyaki sauce, Worcestershire, soy sauce, liquid smoke, ketchup, black pepper and garlic powder in baking dish. Marinate in refrigerator for about 4 to 6 hours.

- When ready to bake, preheat oven to 225° (110° C).

- Discard marinade. Place strips on baking sheet and bake for about 2 to 3 hours or until desired doneness. Serves 4 to 6.

 Adolphus Busch and Otto Koehler started the Lone Star Brewing Company in San Antonio, Texas in 1884.

Irish Corned Beef and Cabbage

Corned Beef and Cabbage is a North Americanized tradition. The most authentic Irish dinner is bacon and cabbage or ham and cabbage.

1 (6 pound) corned beef brisket with spice pack	2.7 kg
6 large onions, sliced, divided	
1 cup malt vinegar	250 ml
½ (12 ounce) bottle Irish stout beer	½ (355 ml)
1 (12 ounce) package baby carrots	340 g
10 - 12 new (red) potatoes, halved	
2 large heads cabbage, quartered	
½ tablespoon black peppercorns	7 ml

■ Preheat oven to 350° (175° C).

■ Place corned beef in large roasting pan and pat spices into meat. Place half of onions around corned beef. Pour vinegar and beer over brisket and add enough water to cover brisket.

■ Cover and bake for 3 hours. Add remaining onions, carrots and new potatoes; top with cabbage.

■ Sprinkle black peppercorns over top. Cover and bake for additional 20 minutes or until vegetables are tender. Serves 10 to 12.

Bacon-Wrapped Brats

4 beef bratwurst	
3 (12 ounce) bottles or cans light beer	3 (355 ml)
½ cup packed brown sugar	110 g
1 teaspoon cayenne pepper	5 ml
6 slices bacon, halved	

- ■ Preheat oven to 425° (220° C).

- ■ Use fork to pierce bratwurst and place in saucepan. Pour beer over top and heat almost to boiling. Reduce heat to low and cook for about 10 to 15 minutes. Remove brats from saucepan and cool to room temperature.

- ■ Mix brown sugar and cayenne. Cut brats into 3 pieces. Wrap each brat with 1 bacon half and secure with toothpick. Coat brats with brown sugar and cayenne mix.

- ■ Line 9 x 13-inch (23 x 33 cm) baking pan with foil and place wire rack in pan. Place wrapped brats on wire rack.

- ■ Bake until bacon is crispy, about 20 to 30 minutes. Serves 4.

 Canned beer was introduced by American Can Company and Krueger Brewing Company of Newark, New Jersey in 1935.

Best Basic Beef Brats

6 - 8 beef bratwurst
2 (12 ounce) bottles or cans beer   2 (355 ml)
Deli or spicy mustard
2 (14 ounce) cans sauerkraut   2 (425 g)

- Place brats in large kettle or soup pot and pour in beer. Cook over medium heat, but not boiling, for about 30 minutes. Remove brats and drain on paper towels.

- Place sauerkraut in saucepan and heat on medium-high. Drain and place in bowl. Serve brats on hot dog buns with spicy mustard and sauerkraut. Serves 6 to 8.

It was as natural as eating and, to me, as necessary. I would not have thought of eating a meal without drinking a beer.
–Ernest Hemingway

Grilled Beer Brats

3 (12 ounce) bottles or cans beer   3 (355 ml)
12 German beef bratwurst
4 onions, sliced thinly
2 green bell peppers, seeded, thinly sliced
2 red bell peppers, seeded, thinly sliced
Oil
Large hot dog buns or sauerkraut and dark bread

■ Mix beer and 1 teaspoon pepper in large ovenproof
  saucepan and heat over medium-high heat until
  steaming, but not boiling. Reduce heat to simmer.

■ Rub brats and vegetables with a little oil and place on
  grill over medium-high heat. Cook until grill marks
  appear and turn. When brats are done and vegetables
  are tender, place all in large saucepan with beer mixture.

■ Cover and heat on low for about 20 to 30 minutes. Warm
  hot dog buns and place brats and vegetables on buns
  or serve on plate with sauerkraut and dark bread. Serve
  immediately with your favorite beer. Serves 8 to 10.

An effective household mosquito spray can be
made from flat beer, antiseptic mouthwash
and Epsom salts. Used in a garden sprayer and
sprayed on areas where mosquitoes swarm, this
homemade mosquito spray is safer than commercial
chemical sprays.

Traditional Irish Stew

1 pound lamb, cubed	455 g
1 (12 ounce) bottle or can beer	355 ml
1 (16 ounce) package baby carrots	455 g
1 pound onions, chopped	455 g
1 pound potatoes, peeled, chopped	455 g
½ teaspoon dried thyme	2 ml

- Place lamb in large stewpot and add enough water to cover three-fourths of meat. Bring water to boil and reduce heat to low. Add beer and cook for about 1 hour. Do not boil after beer is added.

- Add vegetables, thyme, about 1 teaspoon (5 ml) salt and ½ teaspoon (2 ml) pepper and cook until vegetables are tender. Taste and adjust seasonings. Serves 10 to 12.

No soldier can fight unless he is properly fed on beef and beer.
–John Churchill, First Duke of Marlborough

County Goat Roasting

Mesquite split wood logs
1 large gunnysack
1 (10 - 18 pound) suckling goat kid   4.5 - 8.2 kg
Wire
Beer

- Dig pit about 3 feet (1 m) deep and about 3 feet (1 m) wide. Build large mesquite wood fire and burn fire down to make large bed of hot coals.

- Wrap skinned, suckling kid goat in foil, then in wet gunnysack and tie it with wire.

- Place gunnysack on coals, cover with lid of some sort and spread dirt on top. Cook all day.

- Drink beer all day while goat is roasting.

Do you know how the phrase "The Rule of Thumb" got started? It seems that long before the invention of thermometers, brewers tested the temperature of their brews by inserting a thumb. If the liquid was too hot, the yeast would die. So the measurement was critical to the process and became "The Rule of Thumb".

Cabrito

The kitchen method for preparing goat is very simple.

3 - 4 onions, quartered	
¾ cup minced garlic	100 g
1 cup canola oil	250 ml
1 (10 - 18 pound) suckling goat kid,	
quartered	4.5 - 8.2 kg
1 (12 ounce) bottle dark beer	355 ml
1 cup cider vinegar	250 ml
1 (32 ounce) bottle ketchup	910 g
¼ cup yellow mustard	60 g
Juice of small lemon	
1 cup brewed strong black coffee	250 ml
¼ cup chili powder	30 g
1 tablespoon Worcestershire sauce	15 ml

■ Preheat oven to 275° (135° C).

■ Cook onions and garlic in oil in large roasting pan until they are translucent. Add meat and brown. (Add more oil if necessary.) Sprinkle 1 tablespoon (15 ml) pepper over top and pour beer around meat.

■ Mix remaining ingredients in saucepan, heat to boiling and pour over meat.

■ Bake for 2 hours and check liquid; add beer as needed. Bake for additional 1 to 2 hours until meat is tender. Serves 14 to 16.

Amber-Citrus Marinade

2 (12 ounce) bottles amber ale	2 (355 ml)
1 tablespoon red wine vinegar	15 ml
2 tablespoons orange juice	30 ml
1 teaspoon orange zest	5 ml
½ cup canola oil	125 ml
1 tablespoon horseradish sauce	15 ml
½ cup minced onion	80 g
3 - 4 cloves garlic, minced	
1 - 2 teaspoons cayenne pepper	5 - 10 ml

■ Puree all ingredients in blender. Set aside 1 cup (250 ml) for basting meat while cooking.

■ Marinate beef or lamb in refrigerator for several hours before cooking. Discard marinade. Yields about 1 quart (1 L).

Kitchen Sink Sauce for Beef Roast

½ cup barbecue sauce	130 g
½ cup steak sauce	135 g
½ cup balsamic vinegar	125 ml
¼ cup hot sauce	60 ml
1 (12 ounce) bottle or can beer	355 ml
4 cloves garlic, minced	

■ Mix barbecue sauce, steak sauce, balsamic vinegar, hot sauce and beer well.

■ Rub fresh garlic over beef and pat down. Pour sauce over beef, cover and marinate in refrigerator for several hours. Discard marinade. Cook as desired. Yields 2½ cups (625 ml) marinade.

Beer Brisket Sop

Just sop this on a beef brisket when you are grilling or smoking it to keep it moist during the cooking process. Brisket is fork tender when it is well done.

1 onion, minced	
3 cloves garlic, minced	
1 (12 ounce) bottle or can beer	355 ml
¼ cup canola oil	60 ml
¼ cup vinegar	60 ml
2 tablespoons Worcestershire sauce	30 ml
Chili powder	

- Place vegetables in large saucepan with ½ cup (125 ml) water, a little salt and pepper and all remaining ingredients.

- Mix ingredients well and heat on low. Put sop on brisket with pastry brush or rag wrapped around wooden spoon.

- Sop brisket 3 to 4 times while cooking. Yields 1½ cups (375 ml).

Do not cease to drink beer, to eat, to intoxicate thyself, to make love, and to celebrate the good days.
—Ancient Egyptian Credo

Chiquita's Fajita Sauce

1 (8 ounce) bottle Italian salad dressing	250 ml
1 (12 ounce) bottle beer	355 ml
Juice of 3 limes	
1 medium onion, minced	
3 cloves garlic, minced	
3 tablespoons chili powder	25 g
2 tablespoons lemon pepper	30 ml
1 tablespoon Worcestershire sauce	15 ml
2 teaspoons ground cumin	10 ml
1 teaspoon cayenne pepper	5 ml

■ Pour salad dressing and beer in 1-quart (1 L) jar. Add remaining ingredients and shake vigorously. Yields 3 cups (750 ml).

■ Pour over fajita meat and refrigerate for at least 8 hours. Turn several times while marinating. Discard marinade. Yields enough for 2½ pounds (1.1 kg) fajita meat.

Do you know where the phrase "Mind your P's and Q's" came from? Centuries ago in merry old England, pub owners served beer in pints and quarts. When someone got a little unruly, the pub owner scolded the patron by saying, "Mind your P's and Q's!"

Simple Sauce for Meats

1 (12 ounce) bottle or can beer	355 ml
¼ cup snipped parsley	15 g
⅓ cup soy sauce	75 ml
1 tablespoon minced garlic	15 ml

■ Mix all ingredients and pour over meat. Cover and marinate in refrigerator overnight. Turn meat several times.

■ Remove meat and cook as desired. Discard marinade. Yields enough for 1½ to 2 pounds (680 to 910 g) meat.

Stout Barbecue Sauce

½ cup molasses	125 ml
¼ cup mustard	60 g
½ cup chili sauce	135 g
1 teaspoon Worcestershire sauce	5 ml
¼ cup onion flakes	15 g
½ cup oatmeal stout*	125 ml

■ Combine all ingredients in saucepan and heat to almost boiling. Spread over meat and cook as desired.

*TIP: Guinness is the most famous brewer of stout which is a dark, heavy beer that originated in the British Isles. Oatmeal stout is sweeter and has a silky-smooth texture.

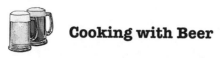
Beer-Battered Chicken Fingers

6 - 8 boneless, skinless chicken breast halves	
1 cup flour	120 g
1 teaspoon baking powder	5 ml
2 eggs, beaten	
½ cup beer	125 ml
1 - 2 cups oil	250 - 500 ml

■ Slice chicken breast halves into 1-inch strips and sprinkle generously with salt and pepper. In separate bowl, mix flour, baking powder, eggs and beer.

■ Coat each chicken strip with batter and carefully place in large skillet of hot oil over medium-high heat. Fry until golden brown on both sides. Drain on paper towels and serve. Serves 8.

 The longest operating brewery in the U.S. was David Yuengling's brewery in Pottsville, Pennsylvania. It operated from 1829 to 1995.

Beer-Sop Grilled Chicken

1 cup (2 sticks) butter	255 g
1 (12 ounce) bottle or can beer	355 ml
1 tablespoon steak seasoning	1 ml
1½ teaspoons seasoned salt	7 ml
6 - 8 boneless, skinless chicken breast halves	
2 red bell peppers, seeded, sliced	

- Mix butter, beer, steak seasoning, seasoned salt and about ½ teaspoon (2 ml) pepper in small skillet over medium-low heat until butter melts and seasonings combine.

- Place chicken on grill over medium-high heat and sear outside of chicken. Reduce heat, spread chicken with sop and baste frequently. Cook until juices run clear. Serves 6 to 8.

WOODY: Little early in the day for a beer, isn't it, Norm?
NORM: So float a corn flake in it.
—Cheers

Cherry-Glazed Chicken

4 boneless, skinless chicken breast halves
Vegetable oil
Butter
6 - 8 green onions with tops, white parts and
    tops diced separately, divided
1 clove garlic, minced
1 (12 ounce) bottle or can beer   355 ml
½ cup chicken broth   125 ml
½ cup dried cherries   60 g
¼ cup half-and-half cream   60 ml
Juice of 1 lemon

- Season chicken generously with salt and pepper. Place in large skillet with oil and butter over medium-high heat and brown on both sides.

- Add white part of green onions (not green tops) garlic and celery to one side of skillet and cook until onions are translucent, about 2 to 3 minutes. Pour beer in slowly and scrape all crusty pieces on pan.

- Spread chicken out, reduce heat and cook on low for about 10 minutes or until liquid reduces to about half.

- Add chicken broth, cherries, cream and lemon juice and cook on low until mixture is steaming hot and juices of chicken run clear. Garnish with green onion tops. Serves 4.

Chicken Italiano

1 (8 ounce) bottle Italian salad dressing	250 ml
¼ teaspoon cayenne pepper	1 ml
4 - 6 boneless, skinless chicken breast halves	
1 (12 ounce) bottle or can beer	355 ml

■ Mix Italian dressing with cayenne pepper and pour over chicken. Cover and refrigerate for at least 3 hours.

■ Discard marinade. Grill chicken over low heat or roast in oven until juices run clear. Pour beer over chicken and refrigerate overnight.

■ Heat before serving. Serves 4 to 6.

Give me a woman who loves beer and I will conquer the world.
—Kaiser Wilhelm, German emperor and King of Prussia

Chicken with Marinara Sauce

6 boneless, skinless chicken breast halves, quartered	
2 tablespoons olive oil	30 ml
1 (28 ounce) can stewed tomatoes	795 g
1 large onion, diced	
1 (8 ounce) carton fresh sliced mushrooms	225 g
2 tomatoes, diced	
1 green bell pepper, seeded, diced	
½ yellow bell pepper, seeded, diced	
1 (10 ounce) can whole kernel corn, drained	280 g
½ cup light beer	125 ml
1 - 2 (8 ounce) packages angel hair pasta	1 - 2 (225 g)

■ Sprinkle chicken generously with salt and pepper. Sear outside of chicken on both sides in oil in large skillet over medium-high heat.

■ Reduce heat and cook for about 5 minutes on both sides. Remove chicken.

■ Combine stewed tomatoes, onion, bell peppers, corn and beer in same skillet and heat almost to boiling point. (Do not boil or beer will turn bitter.)

■ When sauce is very hot and steaming, add chicken and reduce heat to low. Cover and cook for about 1 hour or until juices of chicken run clear.

■ Prepare pasta according to package instructions and serve chicken and sauce over pasta. Serves 4 to 6.

Curried-Tomato Chicken

4 - 6 boneless, skinless chicken breast halves	
2 tablespoons butter	30 g
1 onion, chopped	
½ (12 ounce) bottle or can beer	½ (355 ml)
1 (10 ounce) can tomato soup	280 g
1 teaspoon curry powder	5 ml
½ teaspoon dried basil	2 ml
½ cup grated parmesan cheese	50 g

■ Preheat oven to 350° (175° C).

■ Place chicken in sprayed, 9 x 13-inch (23 x 33 cm) baking dish and sprinkle both sides with salt and pepper. Melt butter in skillet over medium-high heat and saute onion until translucent.

■ Add beer, soup, curry powder and basil to skillet. Reduce heat to low and cook for about 10 minutes or until mixture thickens.

■ Pour sauce over chicken and bake for about 1 hour, until juices run clear. (If they don't, chicken is not cooked.) Sprinkle parmesan over top and bake until cheese melts, about 5 minutes. Serves 4 to 6.

I work until beer o'clock.
—Steven King

Easy Baked Chicken with a Twist

4 skinless, boneless chicken breast halves	
1 teaspoon dried oregano	5 ml
1 cup light beer	250 ml
1 (8 ounce) round Brie cheese, sliced ¼-inch (6 mm) thick	225 g

■ Preheat oven to 350° (175° C).

■ Place chicken breast halves in sprayed baking dish and season with ½ teaspoon salt, a little pepper and oregano. Pour beer into dish and cover.

■ Bake for 1 hour, remove and check to see if juices run clear. If not, bake until juices run clear.

■ After juices run clear, place strips of Brie over top of chicken, return to oven for several minutes until cheese melts. Serves 3 to 4.

Beer is measured by percentage of weight of alcohol per volume. The measurement "3.2%" equals 3.2 grams of alcohol per 100 centiliters of beer. It is about 20% less than liquor.

Easy Sauced Chicken

1 cup beer	250 ml
1 cup soy sauce	250 ml
2 cloves garlic, minced	
4 boneless, skinless chicken breast halves	

■ Combine beer, soy sauce, garlic and 1 cup (250 ml) water in baking dish. Place chicken breast halves in dish and spoon sauce over top. Season with a little salt and pepper.

■ Seal with plastic wrap and refrigerate overnight. Turn once and reseal.

■ Discard marinade and cook chicken on grill over medium-low heat for about 5 to 10 minutes per side or until juices run clear. Do not overcook. Serves 3 to 4.

Whiskey and beer are a man's worst enemies... but the man that runs away from his enemies is a coward!
—Zeca Pagodinho, Brazilian songwriter

Hot Shot Chicken

4 boneless, skinless chicken breast halves	
4 green onions with tops, chopped	
1 teaspoon dried rosemary	5 ml
1 teaspoon dried sage	5 ml
1 teaspoon dried thyme	5 ml
3 cloves garlic, minced	
1 (12 ounce) bottle or can beer	355 ml

■ Preheat broiler.

■ Sprinkle salt and pepper generously over chicken. Place in sprayed baking dish and broil in oven to brown chicken on both sides.

■ Place chicken in sprayed slow cooker and sprinkle with onions, rosemary, sage, thyme and garlic. Pour beer around chicken and cook on LOW for 4 hours. Serves 4.

 It's better to use molasses or maple syrup as a sweetener instead of sugar because the molasses and maple syrup flavors go well with malt flavors.

Mushroom Chicken

4 - 5 boneless, skinless, chicken breast halves
2 (12 ounce) bottles or cans beer, divided   2 (355 ml)
1 cup sliced fresh mushrooms   70 g
2 tablespoons butter, divided   30 g
¼ cup grated parmesan cheese   25 g

- ■ Sprinkle salt and pepper over chicken and place in sprayed baking dish. Pour 1 bottle beer over chicken, cover with plastic wrap and refrigerate for about 45 minutes.

- ■ Saute mushrooms in skillet with 1 tablespoon butter until mushrooms are tender. Remove from skillet.

- ■ Discard marinade, brown chicken on both sides with remaining butter in skillet and cook until juices run clear.

- ■ Reduce heat to medium low, add mushrooms and remaining beer, cover and cook for additional 15 minutes. Remove chicken from skillet, place mushrooms on top and sprinkle with parmesan cheese. Serves 4.

COACH: Can I draw you a beer, Norm?
NORM: No, I know what they look like. Just pour me one.
—Cheers

South-of-the-Border Chicken

1 (12 ounce) bottle pale ale	355 ml
2 limes, divided	
1 teaspoon honey	5 ml
¼ cup chopped cilantro	5 g
4 - 5 boneless, skinless chicken breast halves	

- Mix beer, juice of 1 lime, honey and cilantro in sprayed baking dish and place chicken breast halves in dish. Cover with plastic wrap and refrigerate for 30 minutes, turning once.

- Remove chicken and discard marinade. Sprinkle with salt and pepper and place on hot grill over medium-low heat. Squeeze remaining lime over chicken, turn and continue cooking until juices run clear. (Don't overcook or chicken will dry out.) Serves 4.

We are here to drink beer...
and live our lives so well that
Death will tremble to take us.

—Charles Bukowski, German-American writer

Special Sauce
Barbecued Chicken

½ (12 ounce) bottle or can beer	½ (355 ml)
1 onion, diced	
½ cup ketchup	135 g
1 tablespoon molasses	15 ml
2 cloves garlic, minced	
1 teaspoon seasoned salt	5ml
4 boneless, skinless chicken breast halves	

■ Mix beer, onion, ketchup, molasses, garlic, seasoned salt and a little pepper in bowl.

■ Sprinkle salt and pepper generously over chicken. Place on hot grill over medium-high heat and sear outside of chicken.

■ Reduce heat and baste chicken on both sides. Cook slowly and baste with sauce until juices of chicken run clear. Serves 4

Let us drink for the replenishment of our strength, not our sorrow.
—Cicero

Grilled Chicken Special

1 (12 ounce) bottle or can beer	355 ml
½ cup (1 stick) butter	115 g
2 cloves garlic, minced	
1 tablespoon seasoned salt	15 ml
4 chicken quarters	
Garlic powder	

- Mix beer, butter, garlic, seasoned salt and a little pepper in small saucepan over low heat until butter melts and seasonings combine.

- Place chicken quarters on hot grill over medium-high heat and sear both sides. Reduce heat and baste chicken with beer mixture frequently. Sprinkle garlic powder over coals several times and cook until juices run clear. Serves 4.

The house was as empty as a beer closet in premises where painters have been at work.

—Mark Twain

Orzo Chicken

½ cup orzo pasta	85 g
1 (12 ounce) bottle or can beer	355 ml
¼ cup canola oil	60 ml
1 (1 pound) package boneless, skinless	
chicken thighs	455 g
1 onion, diced	
3 cloves garlic, minced	
½ (14 ounce) can chicken broth	½ (395 g)
1 (6 ounce) can tomato sauce	170 g
1 (2 ounce) can diced pimentos, drained well	55 g
1 tablespoon ground turmeric	15 g

■ Place orzo in bowl and pour beer over pasta. Sprinkle chicken with a little salt and pepper and brown on both sides in large skillet with hot oil over medium-high heat. Reduce heat to medium and cook until juices run clear. Drain chicken and discard oil.

■ Add onions and garlic to skillet and cook until onions are translucent. Add broth, tomato sauce, pimentos and turmeric to orzo-beer mixture and pour over onions and garlic. Add chicken, reduce heat to medium, cover and cook for about 10 minutes.

■ Check seasonings and add salt and pepper, if needed. Serves 4.

Smoke-Gets-in-Your-Eyes Chicken

4 cups mesquite wood chips	1 L
2 (12 ounce) bottles or cans beer	2 (355 ml)
6 chicken-leg quarters, skinned	
1 (10 ounce) bottle barbecue sauce	280 g

■ Soak mesquite wood chips in beer for about 1 hour. Heat grill for medium fire. Add wood chips around edges and some on top of charcoal fire or gas grill that is medium-hot.

■ Place leg quarters on grill and cook for about 5 to 8 minutes or until grill marks show. Turn chicken and cook other side for about 5 to 8 minutes or until grill marks show. (Make sure fire is not too hot or chicken will cook too fast and dry out.)

■ Remove chicken and place each piece on enough foil to completely cover leg quarter. Coat chicken with barbecue sauce on both sides. Wrap and seal edges of foil.

■ Add more mesquite chips around edges. Make sure fire is medium low and place foil packages on grill. Cook for about 20 to 25 minutes or until juices run clear. Serves 4 to 6.

Attention! Chicken

1 (12 ounce) can beer, divided	355 ml
1 (8 ounce) jar dijon-style mustard	225 g
1 (3 pound) chicken	1.4 kg
1 (8 ounce) bottle Italian salad dressing	250 ml

■ Mix half beer and mustard and spread over chicken. Remove any pieces in cavity and spread mustard mixture generously in cavity.

■ Pour Italian dressing in remaining ½ can beer. Place on sturdy baking sheet and position chicken with beer can inside cavity. (Chicken will be sitting up at attention.)

■ Place on grill over medium fire or in oven at 300° (150° C) for about 30 minutes. Baste with any remaining beer-mustard mixture and make sure fire is not too high. Continue cooking until juices run clear, for additional 20 to 30 minutes. Serves 4 to 6.

"Sir, you're drunk!" "Yes, Madam, I am. But in the morning, I will be sober and you will still be ugly."
—Lady Astor and Winston Churchill

Beer-Battered Fried Chicken

1 (2 pound) chicken, cut-up	910 g
2 cups buttermilk*	500 ml
2 eggs, lightly beaten	
½ cup mayonnaise	110 g
⅓ cup amber ale	75 ml
4 cups flour	480 g
Canola oil	

- ■ Sprinkle chicken pieces generously with salt and pepper. Whisk buttermilk and eggs together and add mayonnaise and ale.

- ■ Drop chicken in egg mixture and dredge in flour to coat all sides. Carefully place in hot oil in large skillet over medium-high heat. Brown outside of chicken, reduce heat and cook for about 10 minutes or until juices run clear.

- ■ Drain on paper towels and serve immediately. Serves 4 to 6.

TIP: To make buttermilk, mix 1 cup (250 ml) milk with 1 tablespoon (15 ml) lemon juice or vinegar and let milk stand for about 10 minutes.

 Anheuser-Busch, Miller, Heileman, Stroh, Coors and Pabst are the six largest breweries in the U.S. and control 92% of beer production.

Beer-in-the-Rear Chicken

Straight from The Authorized Texas Ranger Cookbook *by Cheryl and Johnny Harris, this recipe captures the spirit and imagination of retired Texas Ranger Bill Gunn.*

1 whole frying chicken
Olive oil
Rosemary
Thyme
Onion flakes
Garlic flakes
Onion, apple or celery slices
Light beer

- Buy a whole frying-size chicken. This will work equally well on the BBQ pit or in the kitchen oven. You can prepare the chicken to suit individual tastes. You are limited only by your imagination.

- Some suggestions are to rub the chicken with olive oil and sprinkle with rosemary and thyme or sprinkle with onion flakes and garlic flakes (inside and out). Place slice of onion, apple or celery in cavity of chicken.

- After preparing chicken, open a can of light beer (open two or three additional holes in top) and insert can of beer upright into cavity of the chicken. Place upright in shallow pan in oven at 325° (165° C) for 2 hours or until done.

- If barbecuing, place chicken upright on grill (after placing beer can in cavity). Baste with sauce about 30 minutes before done. Serves 4.

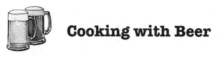
Gingered Chicken Marinade

1 (12 ounce) bottle sweet wheat beer, flat	355 ml
½ cup olive oil	125 ml
2 tablespoons peeled, finely minced ginger	30 ml
2 cloves garlic, minced	
¼ cup orange zest	25 g
6 boneless, skinless chicken breast halves	

- Combine all ingredients (except chicken) in large bowl. Place each breast in marinade and make sure marinade covers.

- Cover and refrigerate for at least 4 hours or overnight. Turn chicken several times while in refrigerator.

- Remove chicken from marinade and discard marinade. Grill both sides of chicken breasts until golden brown and juices run clear. Serves 4 to 6.

The first "brew pub" allowed to make its own beer, serve it on the premises and serve food with it was Yakima Brewing and Malting Company in Yakima, Washington in 1982.

Old-Style Barbecue Sauce

1 (28 ounce) bottle ketchup	795 g
1 (12 ounce) bottle or can beer	355 ml
1 small onion, diced	
1½ cups packed dark brown sugar	330 g
½ cup prepared mustard	125 g
3 tablespoons barbecue seasoning	45 ml
2 tablespoons white vinegar	30 ml
1 teaspoon garlic powder	5 ml

- Mix ketchup, beer, onion, brown sugar, mustard, barbecue seasoning, vinegar, garlic powder and 1 teaspoon (5 ml) pepper in sprayed slow cooker.

- Cover and cook on LOW overnight. Serve over chicken. Yields enough for 3 pounds (1.4 kg).

A fine beer may be judged with only one sip, but it's better to be thoroughly sure.
—Czech proverb

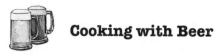

Wasabi-San Barbecue Sauce

1 (12 ounce) bottle amber beer, divided	355 ml
¼ cup honey	85 g
1 (24 ounce) bottle ketchup	680 g
½ cup Worcestershire sauce	125 ml
2 tablespoons lemon juice	30 ml
¼ cup dried wasabi powder	60 ml
3 tablespoons dry mustard	45 ml
1 tablespoon onion powder	15 ml
1 tablespoon ground cumin	15 ml
¼ teaspoon cayenne pepper	1 ml

■ Pour half the beer, honey and ketchup into saucepan and cook over medium-high heat until ingredients mix. Do not boil.

■ Add Worcestershire and lemon juice and stir. Sprinkle remaining ingredients into mixture, stir and simmer for several hours.

■ Add remaining beer when mixture gets thicker than consistency of ketchup. Use to baste chicken during last half of cooking or grilling. Yields enough for 3 pounds (1.4 kg) of meat.

TIP: This is a great marinade for pork, too.

Slow-Cooked Pork Tenderloin

2 large potatoes, peeled, quartered
3 carrots, peeled, quartered
1 large sweet onion, peeled, quartered
2 (1 pound) pork tenderloins · 2 (455 g)
½ (12 ounce) bottle Molson® Canadian lager
    or equivalent · ½ (355 ml)
2 tablespoons white wine vinegar · 30 ml
1 teaspoon garlic salt · 5 ml

- Place potatoes, carrots and onion in sprayed slow cooker. Place tenderloins on top of vegetables.

- Pour in beer, vinegar, garlic salt and a little salt and pepper. Cover and cook on LOW for 4 to 6 hours or until tender. Serves 4 to 6.

From man's sweat and God's love, beer came into the world.
—Saint Arnold of Metz, the Patron Saint of Brewers

Bacon-Flavored Pork Chops

4 slices bacon	
4 green onions with tops, minced	
2 cloves garlic, minced	
4 - 6 (1-inch thick) pork chops	4 - 6 (2.5 cm)
1 tablespoon marjoram, divided	15 ml
½ teaspoon ground allspice	2 ml
6 cups assorted spring greens	330 g
½ cup beer	125 ml
2 tablespoons mustard	30 g

■ Preheat oven to 350° (175° C).

■ Fry bacon crisp in large skillet and drain on paper towels. Add onions and garlic to skillet and cook until translucent.

■ Sprinkle pork chops with 1 teaspoon (5 ml) marjoram, allspice and a little salt and pepper and place in skillet. Brown on both sides over medium-high heat. Remove pork chops to sprayed baking pan and bake for about 10 minutes.

■ Place greens in skillet and heat them just long enough to wilt. Drain on paper towels. Drain most of bacon grease from skillet, but leave all brown pieces and bits of bacon.

■ Pour beer into skillet and scrape all bacon pieces from bottom and sides of skillet. Add mustard, remaining marjoram, and a little salt and pepper and stir slowly. Cook on low, stirring frequently, for about 5 to 10 minutes or until sauce thickens.

■ Serve pork chops on platter with greens and a little sauce on top. Serve sauce on the side. Serves 4 to 6.

Easy Pork Chops

1 (8 ounce) bottle ketchup	225 g
1 (12 ounce) bottle or can beer	355 ml
¾ cup packed brown sugar	165 g
1 tablespoon Worcestershire sauce	15 ml
1 tablespoon lemon juice	15 ml
6 - 8 thin-cut pork chops	

■ Preheat oven to 350° (175° C).

■ Mix ketchup, beer, brown sugar, Worcestershire and lemon juice and pour over pork chops in sprayed 9 x 13-inch (23 x 33 cm) baking pan.

■ Bake for 1 hour. Stir sauce and spoon over pork chops several times. Serves 6 to 8.

Beer makes you feel the way you ought to feel without beer.
–Henry Lawson

Slow-Cooker Chops

2 onions, quartered	
4 (1-inch thick) butterfly-cut pork chops	4 (2.5 cm)
2 gala apples, peeled, quartered	
½ (12 ounce) bottle or can beer	½ (355 ml)
1 (14 ounce) can chicken broth	395 g
1 cup brown rice	185 g

- ■ Place onions in sprayed slow-cooker. Place butterfly pork chops on top of onions

- ■ Place apples on top of pork chops. Pour in beer, chicken broth and rice. Cover and cook on LOW for 6 to 8 hours.

I drink to make other people interesting.
—George Jean Nathan

Grilled Teriyaki Chops

3 ounces lager	90 ml
⅔ cup teriyaki sauce	150 ml
¼ cup cider vinegar	60 ml
¼ cup sweet sherry	60 ml
⅓ cup packed brown sugar	75 g
2 tablespoons chopped, fresh gingerroot	30 ml
6 (1-inch thick) butterfly-cut pork chops	6 (2.5 cm)

■ Pour beer, teriyaki sauce, vinegar, sherry, brown sugar and gingerroot into medium saucepan. Cook on medium-high heat and stir mixture until brown sugar dissolves and sauce reduces to about 1⅓ cups (310 ml).

■ Place pork chops in sprayed 9 x 13-inch (23 x 33 cm) baking dish and pour sauce over chops. Cover with plastic wrap and refrigerate overnight. Turn chops several times to coat both sides of pork.

■ When ready to grill, allow chops to get to room temperature. Discard marinade. Place chops on sprayed grill and cook over medium heat until brown, about 4 to 5 minutes on each side. Cook until chops are just slightly pink inside. Serves 4 to 6.

The first and largest beer tasting and competition was held in Colorado in 1981 and is called the Great American Beer Festival.

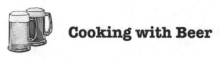

Sassy Pork Chops

4 bone-in center-cut pork loin chops	
Vegetable oil	
¼ cup beer	60 ml
⅓ cup ketchup	90 g
2 tablespoons brown sugar	30 g
2 tablespoons lemon juice	30 ml

■ Season pork chops with a little salt and pepper. Cook chops in large skillet with a little oil until brown on outside and slightly pink on inside.

■ Combine beer, ketchup, brown sugar and lemon juice and pour over chops. Cook on high just until steaming. (Do not boil.)

■ Reduce heat and cook on low; stir frequently until sauce thickens, about 15 to 20 minutes. Remove chops and place on ovenproof dish. Keep warm in oven at 200° (95° C).

■ Cook sauce on low until sauce thickens and reduces by half. Serve with pork chops. Serves 4.

You can never buy beer, you just rent it.
—Archie Bunker

Sauced Chops

4 - 6 (1-inch thick) boneless pork chops	4 - 6 (2.5 cm)
⅓ cup ketchup	90 g
⅓ cup packed brown sugar	75 g
1 teaspoon prepared mustard	5 ml
1 teaspoon onion powder	5 ml
1 (12 ounce) bottle Samuel Adams Boston Lager®, divided	355 ml
Vegetable oil	

■ Season pork chops with a little salt and pepper. Mix ketchup, brown sugar, mustard and onion powder in small bowl to make sauce. Add about half the beer and mix well.

■ Cook pork chops in large skillet with a little oil until brown on the outside and slightly pink inside.

■ Add remaining beer and ketchup-based sauce to pork chops and cook on low until sauce thickens. Serves 4.

Beer is a wholesome liquor...
it abounds with nourishment.
—Dr. Benjamin Rush, American physician

Sam's Sweet Chops

8 thin-cut pork chops	
1 (12 ounce) bottle Samuel Adams	
Boston Lager®	355 ml
2 cups ketchup or barbecue sauce	545 g/530 g
2 cups packed brown sugar	440 g

■ Preheat oven to 350° (175° C).

■ Lay out pork chops in sprayed 9 x 13-inch (23 x 33 cm) baking dish, sprinkle well with salt and pepper and pat down.

■ Mix beer, ketchup and brown sugar in large bowl and pour over chops. Bake for 1 hour or until meat is very tender. Cover with foil if chops begin to turn dark brown. Serves 6 to 8.

 For the best tasting beer, hand-washing all glassware is recommended because it doesn't leave a residue on the glasses like a dishwasher.

Skillet-Barbecued Pork Chops

6 thin-cut pork chops
Seasoned salt
Canola oil
1 (12 ounce) bottle or can lager   355 ml
1 (18 ounce) bottle barbecue sauce   510 g
1 (4 ounce) can diced green chilies   115 g
2 onions, sliced

■ Sprinkle pork chops with seasoned salt and brown both sides in skillet with a little oil.

■ Remove chops. Pour beer into skillet and deglaze pan by scraping sides of skillet.

■ Add barbecue sauce and green chilies, stir and cook on low heat for several minutes. Place chops in skillet.

■ Add onions, cover and continue to cook on low heat for about 1 hour 30 minutes. Serves 4 to 6.

We're wanted men, we'll strike again, but first let's have a beer.
—Jimmy Buffet

Beer-Glazed Pork Roast

1 (2 - 3 pound) boneless pork shoulder roast	910 g - 1.4 kg
3 cloves garlic, minced	
2 tablespoons caraway seeds	30 ml
2 - 3 large onions, sliced	
2 bell peppers, seeded, sliced	
1 (12 ounce) bottle or can beer, cold, divided	355 ml

■ Preheat oven to 450ª (230° C).

■ Place shoulder roast in large roasting pan. Season with a little salt and pepper. Pour in about 1 inch (2.5 cm) water.

■ Pat minced garlic and caraway seeds into roast. Place onions and bell peppers around shoulder. Cover and bake for 30 minutes. Add water if needed at any time while cooking. Reduce heat to 350° (175° C) and bake for 1 hour 30 minutes.

■ Remove roast from oven and pour one-third COLD beer over roast. Bake for additional 30 minutes. After 10 minutes or so, pour one-half remaining COLD beer over roast. After another 10 minutes, pour remaining COLD beer over roast to glaze outside of roast.

■ When meat begins to fall apart, remove from oven and cool. Slice after about 10 to 15 minutes. Serves 6 to 8.

Cheery Barbecue
Pork Ribs

4 pounds baby back pork ribs	1.8 kg
Pinch sugar	
1 tablespoon cracked black pepper	15 ml
2 (16 ounce) bottles barbecue sauce	2 (455 g)
2 - 4 dashes hot sauce	
1 - 2 (12 ounce) bottles porter, room	
temperature	1 - 2 (355 ml)

- Cut ribs apart in 2 to 3-bone pieces. Place in large soup pot or large kettle and cover with water. Sprinkle sugar and black pepper in water and boil for 20 minutes.

- Remove ribs, drain on paper towels and pat dry. Set aside for about 45 minutes.

- Heat gas or charcoal grill. Spread very thin coat of barbecue sauce on ribs and place on grill over high heat. Cook until grill marks show on both sides. (A lot of barbecue sauce on ribs will burn.)

- Remove ribs from grill and place in sprayed slow cooker. Pour remaining barbecue sauce, hot sauce and beer in saucepan and heat on low just long enough to mix well.

- Pour over ribs, cover and cook on LOW for about 5 to 6 hours or until meat falls off bones. Serves 6 to 8.

Hangover Ribs

2 - 3 (2 pound) racks pork spareribs	2 - 3 (910 g)
2 (12 ounce) bottles lager	2 (355 ml)
1½ cups honey	510 g
½ cup barbecue sauce	130 g
1 tablespoon prepared mustard	15 ml
2 teaspoons seasoned salt	10 ml
¼ cup lemon juice	60 ml

- ■ Cut ribs in smaller pieces to fit in sprayed 9 x 13-inch (23 x 33 cm) or larger glass baking dish. Combine remaining ingredients with a little salt and pepper in large bowl and pour over ribs.

- ■ Cover and refrigerate overnight. Turn several times to cover all ribs.

- ■ When ready to cook, discard marinade. Place on grill with medium-hot coals or medium heat for gas grill and cook for about 45 minutes to 1 hour. Turn often and cook slowly. Serves 8 to 12.

Drunk is feeling sophisticated when you can't say it.
—Anonymous

Barbecue Beer Ribs

1½ cups spicy tomato juice cocktail	375 ml
1 cup honey barbecue sauce	265 g
½ (12 ounce) can beer	½ (355 ml)
8 (6 ounce) boneless country-style pork ribs, fat trimmed	8 (170 g)

■ Combine tomato juice cocktail, barbecue sauce and beer in a large resealable plastic bag. Add ribs and turn to coat ribs well. Refrigerate for at least 2 hours or overnight.

■ Discard marinade and throw the ribs on the grill for 15 minutes. Serves 8.

Beer is proof that God loves us and wants us to be happy.
—Benjamin Franklin

Ham It Up

1 (15 ounce) can sliced pineapple	425 g
1 (10 pound) ham shank or butt	4.5 kg
1 (12 ounce) can beer	355 ml

■ Preheat oven to 350° (175° C).

■ Secure pineapple slices to ham in several places with toothpicks. Place ham in large roasting pan with fatty side at top.

■ Pour beer into roasting pan, cover and bake for 3 hours or until ham falls off bone. Serves 6.

Did you know that when Prohibition was rescinded in 1933 beer was left off the list, making it illegal to brew beer at home? It wasn't until 1979 with the Cranston Bill that home brewing of beer was made legal. Somebody forgot the beer in the original Repeal of Prohibition.

Ham Steaks with Beer Sauce

2 - 4 round slices Cure 81® ham	
½ (12 ounce) bottle lager, room temperature	½ (355 ml)
1 tablespoon plus 2 teaspoons cornstarch	25 ml
¼ cup packed brown sugar	55 g
¼ cup raisins	40 g
¼ cup chopped pecans	30 g
1 tablespoon butter	15 ml

- ■ Brown ham slices on both sides in large skillet, wrap in foil and place in oven at 200° (95° C) to keep warm. Mix a little beer and cornstarch in small bowl until cornstarch dissolves.

- ■ Pour beer mixture and remaining beer in saucepan. Add brown sugar, heat on low and stir until brown sugar dissolves.

- ■ Add raisins, pecans and butter and cook until sauce thickens. Serve hot with ham. Serves 4 to 6.

The mouth of a perfectly happy man is filled with beer.
—Ancient Egyptian wisdom

Eggplant-Pasta Specialty

1 (16 ounce) package penne pasta	455 g
1 (1 pound) eggplant, peeled, diced	455 g
¼ - ½ cup olive oil	60 - 75 ml
¾ (12 ounce) bottle lager	¾ (355 ml)
¾ - 1 cup cooked, smoked, cubed ham	105 - 140 g
1 cup frozen peas, thawed	145 g
Grated parmesan cheese	

- Cook pasta according to package directions; drain.

- Cook eggplant in oil over medium heat for about 5 to 8 minutes or until eggplant is almost tender. Stir several times and sprinkle a little salt and pepper over eggplant.

- Pour beer in skillet, add ham and cook over medium-high heat, but do not boil, until liquid reduces by half.

- Add peas and cook for several minutes until peas are hot. Drain and serve immediately with grated parmesan. Serves 4.

Work is the curse of the drinking class.
—Oscar Wilde

Rainbow Brat Kebabs

4 pork bratwurst	
1 (12 ounce) can light beer	355 ml
1 (8 ounce) package button mushrooms	225 g
1 green bell pepper, seeded, quartered	
1 red bell pepper, seeded, quartered	
1 large sweet onion, peeled, quartered	
1 medium zucchini, thick sliced	
1 (6 ounce) carton grape tomatoes	170 g
1 (16 ounce) bottle barbecue sauce	455 g

- Cut brats into bite-size pieces and place in large bowl. Pour beer over brats and marinate for 1 hour.

- Discard marinade. Alternate brat bites with mushrooms, bell peppers, onion, zucchini and tomatoes on skewers.

- Grill over medium fire until brats cook through. Baste frequently with barbecue sauce. Serve immediately. Serves 4.

Many battles have been fought and won by soldiers nourished on beer.
–Frederick the Great

Red, White and Brat

1 large head red cabbage, shredded	
1 large onion, chopped	
2 gala apples, cored, sliced	
¼ cup oil	60 ml
2 tablespoons sugar	25 g
2 tablespoons vinegar	30 ml
½ (12 ounce) bottle or can lager	½ (355 ml)
1 (1 pound) package smoked bratwurst, sliced	455 g
1 (1 pound) package new potatoes, halved	455 g

■ Cook cabbage, onion and apples with oil in large skillet over medium-high heat until cabbage is slightly tender, about 5 minutes.

■ Sprinkle mixture with sugar and vinegar. Pour beer in skillet and place brats and potatoes on top of cabbage mixture. Season with salt and pepper.

■ Turn heat to medium-high and cook for 5 minutes. Reduce heat to medium-low, cover and cook for 30 to 35 minutes or until potatoes are tender in center. Serves 4.

Beer is second only to tea as the world's most popular beverage.

Summertime Brats

6 pork or beef bratwursts or Italian sausages
Olive oil
2 Vidalia® or 1015 Texas SuperSweet
    onions, sliced
½ (12 ounce) bottle or can dark beer   ½ (355 ml)
Buns

- Cook sausages in large skillet with a little olive oil until brown on outside. Drain on paper towels.

- Saute onions in a little olive oil in same skillet until translucent. Place sausages back in skillet.

- Pour in beer, cover and cook on medium for about 20 minutes or until liquid thickens to syrup consistency. Serve immediately on buns. Serves 4 to 6.

Beer — because one doesn't solve the world's problems over white wine.

—Anonymous

Under Cover Dogs

1 large onion, thinly sliced	
1 tablespoon olive oil	30 ml
2 (12 ounce) bottles or cans beer	2 (355 ml)
4 cooked pork or beef bratwurst	
1 tablespoon dijon-style mustard	15 ml
4 (8 inch) flour tortillas, warmed	4 (20 cm)
4 slices cheddar cheese	

- ■ Saute onions in oil in large skillet on medium-low heat for 3 to 5 minutes or until onions are translucent.

- ■ Pour beer into saucepan and bring almost to boil. Add bratwurst, cover and cook for 5 minutes, but do not boil. (Beer will turn bitter if boiled.)

- ■ Drain bratwurst and grill over medium heat until brown; turn occasionally. Spread mustard on tortillas and place cheese, onions and bratwurst on tortilla and roll up. Serve immediately. Serves 4.

 Adrian Block and Hans Christiansen set up the first brewery in the New World in 1612 on the southern tip of Manhattan.

Korny Kielbasa

2 pounds kielbasa sausage	910 g
1 (20 ounce) can sauerkraut, drained	565 g
1 (12 ounce) bottle or can lager	355 ml
2 (8 ounce) packages cornbread muffin mix	2 (225 g)
2 eggs	
⅔ cup milk	150 ml

■ Slice kielbasa in bite-size pieces and place in sprayed slow cooker. Add sauerkraut and beer. Cover and cook on LOW for 5 to 6 hours or until kielbasa cooks completely.

■ Prepare cornbread muffin mix with eggs and milk according to package directions and bake. Cut muffins in half and scoop kielbasa over muffins. Serve immediately. Serves 4.

There are more old drunks than there are old doctors.
–Willie Nelson

Crunchy Fried Fish

1 cup flour	120 g
2 tablespoons paprika	30 ml
1 tablespoon garlic powder	15 ml
1 egg, beaten	
1 (12 ounce) bottle or can beer	355 ml
Oil	
8 - 10 cod or haddock fillets	

- Mix flour, paprika, garlic powder and 1 teaspoon (5 ml) each of salt and pepper in shallow bowl. Add egg and beer, a little at a time, and mix well.

- Heat oil in deep fryer or deep skillet. Dredge fillets in batter and carefully drop into hot oil. Cook until both sides are golden brown and crispy. Remove from oil and drain on paper towels. Serves 4 to 6.

I drink when I have occasion, and sometimes when I have no occasion.

–Miguel de Cervantes

Easy Beer-Battered Fish

1 cup flour	120 g
1 cup flat beer	250 ml
Oil	
4 (2 - 4 ounce) fish fillets	4 (55 - 115 g)

■ Combine flour, a little salt and pepper, and beer in bowl and stir to batter consistency. Pour oil into large skillet and heat over medium-high heat.

■ Carefully place fillets in hot oil and fry until golden brown on both sides. Drain on paper towels and serve hot. Serves 2 to 4.

It is most requisite and fit that the Housewife be experienced and well practiced in the well making of malt... for as from it is made the drink by which the household is nourished and sustained.

–The English Housewife (published 1683)

Southern Fried Catfish

1½ pounds catfish fillets	680 g
1 - 2 (12 ounce) bottles or cans beer	1 - 2 (355 ml)
1 cup cornmeal	160 g
¼ cup flour	30 g
Canola oil	

- ■ Dip fillets in beer, then in mixture of cornmeal, flour, and ½ teaspoon (2 ml) each of salt and pepper and coat well.

- ■ Deep fry in oil for 3 to 4 minutes or pan fry at high heat until golden brown. Turn pan-fried fish once. Serves 4.

In 1919 Congress ratified the 18th Amendment to the U.S. Constitution calling for national prohibition to take effect January 16, 1920.

Oceanside Redfish

2 pounds redfish fillets	910 g
1 (8 ounce) bottle Italian dressing	250 ml
1 (12 ounce) bottle or can beer	355 ml
Several dashes hot sauce	

- ■ Place fish in glass baking dish. Pour Italian dressing, beer and hot sauce over fish. Cover and marinate in refrigerator for at least 2 hours.

- ■ When ready to cook, drain fish, discard marinade and place in microwave-safe dish.

- ■ Microwave fish for about 3 to 4 minutes per pound. Be careful not to overcook. Serves 8.

*You're not drunk if you can lie
on the floor without holding on.*
—Dean Martin

Beer-Roasted Salmon

1 (1½ pounds) salmon fillets	680 g
3 - 4 cloves garlic, minced	
2 tablespoons brown sugar	30 g
¼ cup (½ stick) butter	115 g
1 small red onion, minced	
1 (12-ounce) bottle or can beer	355 ml
¼ cup chopped almonds	40 g

■ Line 9 x 13-inch (23 x 33 cm) baking pan with foil. Spray foil and place salmon on top.

■ Sprinkle minced garlic and brown sugar over salmon. Drop dabs of butter over top. Sprinkle minced onion over butter.

■ Pour beer into pan and cover with foil. Place baking pan on hot grill and close the lid. Cook for 5 minutes, remove foil and return pan to grill. Cover grill and cook for several minutes until salmon cooks through and is flaky. Serves 4 to 6.

When George Washington was named Commander of the Continental Army, one of his first orders provided for a quart of beer as part of the daily rations for the soldiers.

Hobo Snappers

4 (6 ounce) red snapper fillets	4 (170 g)
3 - 4 red potatoes, thinly sliced	
2 red bell peppers, seeded, chopped	
1 bunch green onions with tops, chopped	
2 teaspoons garlic salt	10 ml
½ cup (1 stick) butter	225 g
1 (12 ounce) bottle or can light beer	355 ml

■ Place 1 fillet on large piece of heavy foil. Layer one-fourth of potatoes, one-fourth bell peppers and one-fourth green tops over fillet. Sprinkle with garlic salt.

■ Dot with butter and pour one-fourth beer over ingredients. Fold foil in such a way to seal so package will not leak.

■ Repeat steps to prepare 3 more packages. Place on grill over medium-high heat for about 5 minutes. Move to cooler place on grill and "steam" for additional 3 to 4 minutes. Serves 4.

Life is too short to drink cheap beer.
—Anonymous

Beer-Drinking Lobsters

2 (12 ounce) bottles or cans light beer   2 (355 ml)
4 whole lobster tails
2 large lemons, sliced
1 (1 pound) package butter, melted   455 g

■ Pour beer into steamer pot and drop several lemon slices in. Heat over medium-high until steaming. (Do not boil.)

■ If lobsters are in shells, cut shell lengthwise on underneath side. Drop lobster tails in steamer basket in steamer pot.

■ Cook until tails turn red. Do not overcook or lobster will be tough. Serve immediately with melted butter and lemon slices. Serves 4.

In Babylonia some four thousand years ago, it was customary for the father of the bride to present his son-in-law with all the honey beer (mead) he could drink for the first month of the marriage. This was considered a part of the bride's dowry. Thus was born the tradition of the honey month or honeymoon as we call it today.

Sunday Special
Scallop Fritters

Oil	
¾ cup cornmeal	120 g
¾ cup flour	90 g
1 tablespoon baking powder	15 ml
¼ cup pilsner beer	60 ml
¼ cup bottled clam broth	60 m
2 eggs	
1 (4 ounce) can diced green chilies, drained	115 g
¼ cup minced celery	25 g
5 green onions with tops, chopped	
½ pound sea scallops, chopped	225 g
Vegetable oil	

■ Mix cornmeal, flour, baking powder, and a little salt and pepper in bowl. Add beer and clam broth a little at a time and stir after each addition.

■ Lightly beat eggs and add to batter mixture. Add green chilies, celery and green onions and stir well. If mixture is too thick for batter consistency, add a little more beer. (It should be thick enough and sticky enough to hold together in a ball.) Gently fold in scallops.

■ Heat oil in deep fryer or large skillet. Carefully drop tablespoonfuls of batter into hot oil and cook until golden, about 5 minutes.

■ Remove with slotted spoon and drain on paper towels. Serves 6.

Seaside Mussels

2 (12 ounce) bottles or cans beer, divided	2 (355 ml)
4 pounds fresh mussels	1.8 kg
½ cup diced celery	50 g
¼ cup minced green onions with tops	25 g
¼ cup chopped red bell pepper	35 g
5 - 6 small sprigs parsley	

■ Scrub mussels to remove all sand and grit. Discard any open ones. Rinse thoroughly and drain on paper towels. Place washed, cleaned mussels in large stock pot.

■ Pour enough beer over mussels to cover or almost cover. Pour celery, green onions, bell pepper and parsley into pot.

■ Cover, heat on medium-high (but do not boil) and steam mussels for about 5 minutes or until mussels open. Discard mussels that do not open.

■ Place mussels in serving bowl. Pour some stock and most of vegetables in serving bowl. Serves 4 to 6.

Because brewing was considered a cooking process, the earliest known brewers in Mesopotamia as well as other ancient cultures were women.

Beer-Battered Shrimp

¾ cup beer, room temperature	175 ml
1 cup flour	120 g
1 large egg, slightly beaten	
½ teaspoon lemon pepper	2 ml
1 pound uncooked shrimp, cleaned	455 g
Vegetable oil	

- Pour beer, a little at a time, into flour and stir to reach batter consistency. Add egg and lemon pepper and stir.

- Dredge shrimp through batter to coat. Carefully place in hot oil of deep fryer and cook until golden brown. Serves 3 to 4.

Here's to the man drinks water pure
and goes to bed quite sober.
He will fall as the leaves will fall,
he'll die before October.
Here's to the man who drinks pale ale
and goes to bed quite mellow.
He does live as he ought to live
and he's a jolly good fellow.

¬Old English drinking song

Crunchy Garlic Shrimp

2 (12 ounce) bottles or cans beer, room temperature	2 (355 ml)
2 cups flour	240 g
2 teaspoons garlic powder	10 ml
2 pounds medium shrimp, peeled, veined	910 g
Vegetable oil	

- Combine beer, flour, garlic powder, and a little salt and pepper in bowl and stir until it reaches batter consistency. Dip shrimp into batter to cover and carefully place in deep fryer in hot oil.

- Fry until golden brown. Drain on paper towels. Serve immediately. Serves 4 to 6.

Hops were first used in the brewing process in Germany in the 8th century. By the 16th century, almost all beers were brewed with hops. Prior to that time, a mixture of herbs called gruit was used in brewing. A few microbreweries today have revived the production of unhopped beers.

Spicy Coconut Shrimp

1¼ cups flour	150 g
1 tablespoon baking powder	15 ml
1 teaspoon sugar	5 ml
¼ cup plus 1 teaspoon Creole seasoning, divided	50 g/5 ml
4 eggs, lightly beaten	
1 cup beer	250 ml
4 dozen fresh shrimp with tails, peeled, veined	
2 cups shredded coconut	170 g
Oil	

- ■ Mix flour, baking powder, sugar, 1 teaspoon Creole seasoning and a little salt and pepper in bowl. Mix in eggs and beer and stir. Sprinkle remaining Creole seasoning over shrimp.

- ■ Dredge shrimp through batter mixture and then coconut. Heat oil in deep fryer to almost boiling and carefully drop shrimp into oil.

- ■ Fry until golden brown on both sides. Remove from fryer and drain on paper towels. Serves 4 to 6.

 While barley is the most common grain used in brewing, rice is gaining popularity, particularly in the production of American lagers.

Beer-Steamed Shrimp

4 pounds medium shrimp with shells	1.8 kg
2 - 3 (12 ounce) bottles or cans beer	2 - 3 (355 ml)
½ cup chopped celery	50 g
½ cup chopped onion	80 g
½ cup chopped green bell pepper	75 g
3 lemons, divided	
½ cup pickling spice	125 ml
Melted butter or cocktail sauce	

- Rinse shrimp and place in large kettle or soup pot. Pour beer into pot to cover shrimp. Add celery, onion, bell pepper, juice of 2 lemons and pickling spice.

- Bring pot to almost boiling, but do not boil. Steam until shrimp turn pink. Remove from pot and drain on paper towels.

- Serve hot with melted butter and lemon slices or cold with cocktail sauce. Serves 6 to 8.

The science of chemistry as it relates to fermentation (beer brewing, winemaking, yeast, etc.) is called zymurgy. (Zymurgy is also the last word definition in many dictionaries.)

Fisherman's Beer Shrimp

2 (12 ounce) bottles or cans beer	2 (355 ml)
½ cup pickling spice	125 ml
2 lemons, sliced	
2 pounds shrimp	910 g
Butter, melted	

- Pour beer in large saucepan or stew pot over medium-high heat. Add pickling spice and several lemon slices.

- Add shrimp and cook until shrimp changes color. Remove from pot with slotted spoon and drain on paper towels. Serve with melted butter and lemon slices. Serves 4.

Sometimes when I reflect on all the beer I drink I feel ashamed. Then I look into the glass and think about the workers in the brewery and all of their hopes and dreams. If I didn't drink this beer, they might be out of work and their dreams would be shattered. Then I say to myself, "It is better that I drink this beer and let their dreams come true than be selfish and worry about my liver."

—Jack Handy

Bratwurst-Shrimp Boil

1½ pounds beef or pork bratwursts	680 g
2 (12 ounce) bottles or cans beer, room temperature	2 (355 ml)
¾ cup crab boil seasoning	175 ml
2 onions, sliced	
2 lemons, divided	
2 pounds small new potatoes	910 g
8 - 10 half ears corn	
1 pound shrimp with tails, peeled, veined	455 g
Butter, melted	

- Cook brats on grill or in skillet to brown. Pour beer and enough water to cover shrimp (but do not add shrimp) in large 10-quart (10 L) pot and bring almost to boil. (Do not boil.)

- Add crab boil seasoning, onions, juice of 1 lemon, potatoes and corn and cook almost to done. Cut brats into thirds and carefully place in soup pot.

- Add shrimp and steam until shrimp turn pink. Serve with lemon slices and melted butter. Serves 6.

 A labeorphile is a person who collects beer bottles and/or beer labels.

Shrimp Kebabs

1 (12 ounce) bottle or can beer	355 ml
2 tablespoons oil	30 ml
1 tablespoon Worcestershire sauce	15 ml
¼ teaspoon hot sauce	1 ml
2 cloves garlic, minced	
1 (16 ounce) package grape tomatoes	455 g
1 - 2 sweet onions, quartered	
3 - 4 bell peppers, seeded, quartered	
2 pounds large shrimp with tails,	
peeled, veined	910 g
Melted butter	
Cocktail sauce	

■ Pour beer, oil, Worcestershire sauce, hot sauce and garlic in large resealable plastic bag and shake to mix.

■ Add shrimp to marinade, shake bag to coat shrimp and refrigerate for several hours.

■ When ready to cook, run skewer through neck and tail of shrimp. Skewer 1 tomato, 1 piece of onion and 1 piece of bell pepper. Repeat process for rest of skewers.

■ Preheat broiler

■ Place each skewer in sprayed large baking pan. Broil on both sides until shrimp change color. Serve immediately with melted butter and cocktail sauce. Serves 6 to 8.

TIP: It's just as easy to grill kebabs.

Stout-Marinated Shrimp

2 cups olive oil	500 ml
2 (12 ounce) bottles Guinness® Extra Stout	2 (355 ml)
2 jalapeno peppers, seeded*	
4 cloves garlic, quartered	
2 small onions, quartered	
½ cup honey	170 g
2 bunches cilantro, stemmed	
20 fresh jumbo shrimp, shelled, veined	

■ Place all ingredients except shrimp into blender and liquefy. Place shrimp in flat-bottomed dish and pour marinade over top of shrimp. Refrigerate for about 1 hour and stir several times.

■ Place shrimp on hot grill over medium heat. Grill until grill marks show and shrimp turn color. Don't overcook. Serves 4.

TIP: Wear rubber gloves when handling jalapenos.

Guinness is perhaps the most famous beer in the world. Its St. James Gate Brewery in Dublin, Ireland was founded in 1759 and the first beer produced there was a stout.

Tropical Marinade

½ cup (1 stick) butter	115 g
6 - 8 green onions with tops, chopped	
4 - 5 cloves garlic, minced	
1 (12 ounce) bottle or can beer	355 ml
1 lemon	
1 lime	
1 orange	
¼ cup teriyaki sauce	60 ml

■ Heat butter in saucepan over medium heat and cook green onions and garlic until they are translucent. Pour in beer, juice of lemon, juice of lime, juice of orange and teriyaki sauce.

■ Heat marinade and cook on low or simmer for about 30 minutes. Cool to room temperature and pour over seafood.

■ Marinate in refrigerator for about 20 minutes. Yields enough to marinate 4 servings of fish.

TIP: This marinade is great for chicken, too. Marinate chicken for 1 hour.

Fermentation may have been a greater discovery than fire.
–David Rains Wallace

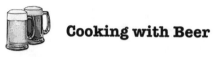

Gale-Force Seafood Sop

1 cube chicken bouillon	
1 (12 ounce) bottle lager	355 ml
¾ cup fresh lime juice (about 6 medium limes)	175 ml
6 garlic cloves, minced	
1 tablespoon hot sauce	15 ml
1 teaspoon Worcestershire sauce	5 ml
1 teaspoon soy sauce	5 ml
1 teaspoon ground black pepper	5ml

■ Dissolve chicken bouillon cube according to package directions. Mix with remaining ingredients and refrigerate for several hours before using.

■ Dab onto seafood while grilling or cooking. Yields enough for 4 fillets.

Light summer beers, like Samuel Adams Summer Ale and Blue Moon, are well suited to grilled seafood, chicken and shellfish. Pale ales, Hefeweizens or pilsners are excellent for sauces and dressings. Hefeweizens and wheat beers are great for steaming hot dogs.

Sweets

Cakes, Cookies & Desserts

New Year's Eve and New Year's Day

New Year's Eve is celebrated by every society using their cultural definitions of the beginning of a new year or a new time. Whether the New Year is marked by a harvest season, moon phases or the Gregorian calendar, the New Year is cause for celebration and renewal.

New Year's Eve and New Year's Day

The final day of the year in the Gregorian calendar, December 31, is a night to ring out the old and ring in the new for countries around the world who celebrate on this night.

Ringing out the old and ringing in the new is not new to man. It's been celebrated for thousands of years.

If you have ever wondered why there are fireworks, noise-makers and revelry on this particular night, you can find their origins written in pyramids, cliff dwellings, ancient texts and legends passed down through the ages.

Wild drink and merriment originally represented the chaotic world before God created today's world.

Traditional noise-makers, horns, whistles and sirens all started with ancient societies who gathered to scare away evil spirits and to create as much havoc as possible.

Fireworks came along for the same reason and today most countries around the world celebrate New Year's Eve with fireworks.

Symbolically, the New Year represented renewal of life, regeneration and starting anew. To Native Americans, the New Year was defined by the harvests. The Creek Indians celebrated the New Year with the ripening of the first corn in July and the new year began in August.

The Dutch in New Amsterdam made beer a central part of the New Year in the New World and also set New Year's Day as the most important holiday because it was celebrated with family and meant hope in the future.

Continued next page...

Continued from previous page...

Resolutions were made first in New York because of the tradition of clearing out one's debts at the end of the year.

Even lucky foods have found their way into New Year's traditions. Black-eyed peas, cabbage, pork, rice and even doughnuts in Dutch circles are required eating on New Year's Day.

Check out some of these great drinks to ring in the New Year and to make it a celebration to remember.

If you want to thicken a dessert that will be refrigerated after beer is added, use unflavored gelatin. One tablespoon (¼ ounce) unflavored gelatin will congeal 2½ cups liquid. Mix the amount of gelatin you think you'll need with about 2 tablespoons water in separate bowl, stir to dissolve and add to your recipe. (Beer should be room temperature.)

Crazy Cinnamon Cake

1 (18 ounce) box spice cake mix	510 g
1 (3 ounce) package instant vanilla pudding mix	85 g
2 teaspoons ground cinnamon	10 ml
¼ cup packed brown sugar	55 g
4 eggs, slightly beaten	
¼ cup oil	60 ml
1 cup beer	250 ml
¾ cup chopped pecans	85 g

■ Preheat oven to 350° (175° C).

■ Combine cake mix, pudding mix and cinnamon in large bowl. Cream brown sugar, eggs, oil and beer in separate bowl.

■ Pour brown sugar-beer mixture into dry cake mixture a little at a time and beat after each addition. Batter should be smooth and creamy. Fold in pecans.

■ Pour into sprayed, floured bundt pan and bake for about 50 minutes until toothpick inserted in center comes out clean. Cool before serving. Serves 12 to 16.

TIP: Dust with powdered sugar if you like.

 The distinctive red triangle logo of the Bass Brewery (famous for its pale ale) is the world's first trademark. It was registered in 1875.

Dad's Oatmeal Cake

½ cup beer	125 ml
1 cup quick-cooking oats	80 g
½ cup (1 stick) butter, softened	115 g
2 cups packed brown sugar	440 g
½ teaspoon vanilla	2 ml
2 eggs, slightly beaten	
1½ cups flour	180 g
1 teaspoon baking soda	5 ml
½ teaspoon ground nutmeg	2 ml
1 teaspoon ground cinnamon	5 ml

■ Preheat oven to 350° (175° C).

■ Heat beer to steaming hot, but not boiling, in small saucepan. Pour over quick-cooking oats, stir and set aside. Cream butter, brown sugar, vanilla and eggs in large bowl.

■ Combine flour, baking soda, nutmeg, cinnamon and ¼ teaspoon (1 ml) salt in separate bowl. Add flour mixture to butter mixture a little at a time and stir well after each addition.

■ Add quick-cooking oats mixture and mix well. Pour batter into sprayed, floured 9 x 13-inch (23 x 33 cm) baking pan and bake for about 30 minutes or until toothpick inserted in center comes out clean. Serves 12 to 16.

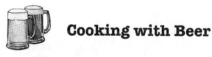

Fruity Spice Cake

1 cup (2 sticks) butter, softened	225 g
2 cups packed dark brown sugar	440 g
2 eggs	
3 cups flour	360 g
2 teaspoons baking soda	10 ml
1 teaspoon ground cinnamon	5 ml
½ teaspoon ground cloves	2 ml
2 cups chopped dates	300 g
1 (12 ounce) bottle or can beer	355 ml
Powdered sugar	

- Preheat oven to 350° (175° C).

- Cream butter and brown sugar in large bowl until smooth. Add eggs, one at a time, and beat well after each addition.

- Combine flour, baking soda, cinnamon, cloves and ¼ teaspoon (1 ml) salt in separate bowl. Pour flour mixture and beer alternately into butter mixture a little at a time and beat after each addition.

- Sprinkle a little flour over dates and stir into batter. Pour into sprayed, floured bundt pan. Bake for about 1 hour until toothpick inserted in center comes out clean.

- Cool and sprinkle top with powdered sugar. Serves 12 to 16.

Autumn Spice Cake

½ cup (1 stick) butter, softened	115 g
1 cup packed brown sugar	220 g
1 egg, beaten	
1½ cups flour	180 g
1 teaspoon ground cloves	5 ml
1 teaspoon ground cinnamon	5 ml
1 teaspoon ground allspice	5 ml
1 teaspoon baking powder	5 ml
½ teaspoon baking soda	2 ml
1 cup beer	250 ml

■ Preheat oven to 375° (190° C).

■ Cream butter and brown sugar until smooth. Add beaten egg and beat until light and fluffy. Combine flour, cloves, cinnamon, allspice, baking powder, baking soda and ¼ teaspoon (1 ml) salt in separate bowl.

■ Mix flour mixture and beer alternately into butter mixture a little at a time and mix after each addition. Pour batter into sprayed, 9 x 5-inch (23 x 13 cm) loaf pan and bake for 40 minutes or until toothpick inserted in center comes out clean. Serves 8 to 10.

 The first known written recipe was for beer. It was recorded on a Sumerian clay tablet some 8,000 years ago.

Easy Bake Bundt Cake

1 (18 ounce) package yellow cake mix	510 g
1 (4 ounce) package instant vanilla	
pudding mix	115 g
1 cup light beer	250 ml
¼ cup oil	60 ml
4 eggs	

■ Preheat oven to 350° (175° C).

■ Stir together cake mix and pudding mix in large bowl. Slowly pour in beer and oil, a little at a time, and mix.

■ Add eggs and beat until mixture is creamy with no lumps. Pour into sprayed bundt pan. Bake for 55 minutes or until toothpick inserted in center comes out clean.

■ Cool on wire rack. Frost with prepared icing, if desired. Serves 12 to 16.

It is believed that barley was probably the first grain that was deliberately cultivated by mankind. Some evidence seems to indicate that the first farming was primarily for providing grain for brewing beer rather than as a food supply.

Guinness Chocolate Cake

½ cup (1 stick) plus 2 tablespoons butter	140 g
1 cup Guinness® stout	250 ml
2 cups sugar	400 g
¼ cup cocoa	20 g
2 large eggs	
¼ cup plus 2 tablespoons sour cream	90 g
1 tablespoon vanilla	15 ml
2 cups flour	240 ml
2½ teaspoons baking soda	12 ml

- Preheat oven to 350° (175°).

- Melt butter in large saucepan over low heat and remove from heat. Pour Guinness® in saucepan, add sugar and cocoa and whisk together.

- Combine eggs, sour cream and vanilla in bowl and mix well. Add to butter-sugar mixture and stir. Add flour and baking soda and stir mixture until smooth.

- Pour into sprayed, floured 9-inch (23 cm) cake pan and bake for 45 minutes to 1 hour until toothpick inserted in center comes out clean. Cool cake in pan.

Frosting:

1¼ cups powdered sugar	150 g
1 (8 ounce) container cream cheese, softened	225 g
½ cup whipping cream	125 ml

- Blend powdered sugar to break up lumps, add cream cheese and blend until smooth. Add whipping cream and mix until frosting is easy to spread.

- Loosen sides of cake pan with knife. Place plate or platter on top of cake pan and turn both over at one time. Remove cake pan and spread frosting on top.

- Cake will look like a glass of Guinness® with frothy head on top. Serves 6 to 8.

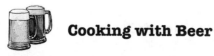

Surprise Chocolate Cake

1½ cups flour	180 g
½ cup cocoa	40 g
1 teaspoon baking soda	5 ml
1¼ cups sugar	250 g
¼ cup canola oil	60 ml
1 tablespoon white cider vinegar	15 ml
2 teaspoons vanilla	10 ml
1 cup light beer	250 ml

■ Preheat oven to 350° (175° C).

■ Combine flour, cocoa, baking soda and pinch of salt in large bowl. In separate bowl mix sugar, oil, vinegar and vanilla. Add beer and stir carefully.

■ Pour flour mixture into sugar-beer mixture a little at a time and mix carefully. Batter should be smooth and creamy.

■ Pour batter into sprayed, floured 8-inch (20 cm) cake pan and bake for 25 minutes until toothpick inserted in center comes out clean. Cool and serve. Serves 6 to 8.

TIP: Top with prepared frosting or powdered sugar if you want it to be sweeter.

The unofficial patron saint of beer is known as King Gambrinus who, legend says, was a king of Flanders, now part of Belgium, the world capital of brewing.

Beer Lover's
Chocolate Cake in a Mug

½ cup flour	60 g
½ cup sugar	100 g
¼ cup cocoa	20 g
2 eggs	
¼ cup milk	60 ml
2 tablespoons beer	30 ml
½ cup canola oil	60 ml
½ cup chocolate chips	85 g
1 teaspoon vanilla	15 ml

■ Mix all ingredients in bowl and pour into 2 large coffee mugs. Put on microwave turntable and microwave for 3 minutes. (If there's no turntable, turn by hand every minute or so.)

■ Cake will rise above edge of mug, but it will be okay. Serves 2.

Of Doctors and medicines we have plenty more than enough... what you may, for the love of God, send is some large quantity of beer.

–Dispatch to London from the New South Wales colony in Australia, 1854

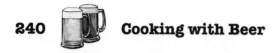

Yummy Chocolate Cupcakes

2½ cups flour	300 g
2 cups sugar	400 g
¾ cup cocoa	60 g
1½ teaspoons baking soda	7 ml
1 (12 ounce) bottle Guinness® stout	355 ml
⅔ cup oil	150 ml
1 tablespoon vanilla	15 ml
3 large eggs	
1 (8 ounce) carton sour cream	225 g

- ■ Preheat oven to 350° (175° C).

- ■ Mix flour, sugar, cocoa, baking soda and 1 teaspoon (5 ml) salt in medium bowl. In separate bowl, combine stout, oil and vanilla. Add eggs, 1 at a time, and beat after each addition. Add sour cream and mix well.

- ■ Pour dry ingredients a little at a time into beer-egg mixture. Pour batter evenly into 24 sprayed or paper-lined muffin cups.

- ■ Bake for 25 minutes or until toothpick inserted in center comes out clean. Cool.

Frosting:

1 (8 ounce) carton cream cheese, softened	225 g
⅓ cup whipping cream	75 ml
1 (16 ounce) box powdered sugar	455 g
2 tablespoons cocoa	10 g

- ■ Beat cream cheese in bowl until light and fluffy. Add whipping cream a little at a time and beat. Slowly pour in powdered sugar and beat until creamy and smooth.

- ■ Spread frosting on each cupcake. Sprinkle cocoa over cupcakes. Yields 24 cupcakes.

Happy Halloween Cookies

3 cups flour	360 g
1 teaspoon baking soda	5 ml
2 teaspoons pumpkin pie spice	10 ml
1 cup (2 sticks) unsalted butter	225 g
1 cup packed brown sugar	220 g
2 cups sugar	400 g
2 large eggs	
1 teaspoon vanilla	5 ml
1 (12 ounce) bottle Guinness® Draught	355 ml
2 cups semi-sweet chocolate chips	340 g
1¼ cups shelled pumpkin seeds	175 g

■ Preheat oven to 325° (165° C).

■ Mix flour, baking soda, 1 teaspoon (5 ml) salt and pumpkin pie spice in large bowl. In separate bowl, beat butter, brown sugar and sugar on medium until creamy and smooth.

■ Add eggs and vanilla to sugar mixture and mix well. Slowly pour in beer while beating on low. Add dry ingredients a little at a time and mix well after each addition. Fold in chocolate chips and pumpkin seeds and stir well.

■ Drop small spoonfuls batter on baking sheet and bake for about 12 to 14 minutes or until brown. Yields about 3 dozen cookies.

Crazy Nutty Cookies

½ cup (1 stick) butter, softened	115 g
1 cup packed brown sugar	220 g
2 cups flour	240 g
1 teaspoon ground cinnamon	5 ml
½ teaspoon baking soda	2 ml
1¼ cups beer, flat	310 ml
½ cup walnut halves	60 g

■ Preheat at 350° (175° C).

■ Cream butter and brown sugar in large bowl. Combine flour, cinnamon and baking soda in separate bowl. Gradually pour flour mixture into butter-sugar mixture and stir well after each addition.

■ Pour beer in and blend carefully. Drop scoops of cookie dough onto sprayed large cookie sheet. Top each scoop with 1 walnut half.

■ Bake for 10 minutes and check color. Bake a few more minutes if needed until cookies are slightly brown on top. Cool on wire rack. Yields 2 dozen cookies.

The word bridal is derived from the phrase bride's ale. This referred to the medieval practice of brides brewing ale to be sold on their wedding day to help defray the costs.

Johnny Apple Rings

1½ cups flour	180 g
¼ cup sugar	50 g
1 (12 ounce) bottle or can pale ale	355 ml
2 tablespoons butter, melted	30 g
1 teaspoon vanilla	5 ml
8 large gala or Granny Smith apples	
Vegetable oil	
Cinnamon	
Powdered sugar	

■ Mix flour and sugar and whisk in beer slowly. Add butter and vanilla and stir.

■ Peel and core apples. Cut thick apple slices horizontally so hole will be in middle to make apple rings.

■ Dry rings on paper towels and dip into batter. Carefully drop rings into hot oil in deep fryer and cook until golden brown on both sides. Drain on paper towels, sprinkle with cinnamon and powdered sugar and serve hot. Serves 6 to 8.

*Sir, if you were my husband,
I would poison your drink.*

–Lady Astor to Winston Churchill

*Madam, if you were my wife,
I would drink it.*

–His reply

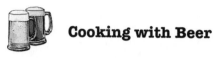

Frozen Apricot Custard

1 (12 ounce) bottle Pyramid apricot ale	355 ml
1 (8 ounce) jar apricot preserves	225 g
1 large egg	
1 cup sugar	200 g
½ cup milk	125 ml
2 cups whipping cream	500 ml

■ Heat ale and apricot preserves in saucepan on medium and stir. Cook on low until sauce is reduced to 1½ cups (375 ml). Remove from heat.

■ Mix egg and sugar in separate bowl. Add milk and whisk together. Slowly pour into saucepan with sauce and stir.

■ Add cream and stir. Refrigerate mixture for about 1 hour. Freeze in ice cream maker according to manufacturer's directions. Yields about 2 quarts.

Stout Mocha Freeze

1 quart coffee ice cream, softened	945 ml
1 cup stout	250 ml
1 cup grated dark semi-sweet chocolate	100 g

■ Place ice cream in large mixing bowl or blender and pour in stout and grated chocolate. Blend until smooth and creamy.

■ Pour into 8 (1 cup/250 ml) bowls and freeze until solid. Serve immediately. Serves 8.

Vanilla Porter Milkshake Treat

4 - 5 scoops vanilla ice cream, softened
½ (12 ounce) bottle or can Breck Brew
    Vanilla Porter   ½ (355 ml)

■ Place all ingredients in blender and process until smooth. Pour in large glass. Yields 1 milkshake.

No-Kidding... Beer Popsicles!

3 (12 ounce) bottles or cans beer   3 (355 ml)
1 popsicle mold tray
Popsicle sticks

■ Open beer and set it aside for at least 24 hours.

■ Pour beer into popsicle molds and insert sticks. Freeze for about 12 hours or until popsicles are solid.

TIP: The exact amount of beer depends on the size of the popsicle molds.

Pabst Blue Ribbon beer got its name because it was awarded a blue ribbon at the Columbian World Exposition (World's Fair) in Chicago, Illinois in 1893.

Index

W

Y

Z

Cookbooks Published by Cookbook Resources, LLC
Bringing Family and Friends to the Table

Easy Diabetic Recipes

The Best of Cooking
with 3 Ingredients

The Ultimate Cooking
with 4 Ingredients

Easy Cooking with 5 Ingredients

Gourmet Cooking with 5 Ingredients

4-Ingredient Recipes
for 30-Minute Meals

Essential 3-4-5 Ingredient Recipes

The Best 1001 Short, Easy Recipes

1001 Slow Cooker Recipes

1001 Short, Easy, Inexpensive Recipes

1001 Fast Easy Recipes

1001 Community Recipes

Busy Woman's Quick & Easy Recipes

Busy Woman's Slow Cooker Recipes

Easy Slow Cooker Cookbook

Easy One-Dish Meals

Easy Potluck Recipes

Easy Casseroles

Easy Desserts

Sunday Night Suppers

Easy Church Suppers

365 Easy Meals

365 Easy Soups and Stews

365 Easy Vegetarian Recipes

365 Easy Casserole Recipes

365 Easy Chicken Recipes

365 Easy Soup Recipes

365 Easy One-Dish Recipes

365 Easy Pasta Recipes

365 Easy Slow Cooker Recipes

Quick Fixes with Cake Mixes

Kitchen Keepsakes &
More Kitchen Keepsakes

Gifts for the Cookie Jar

All New Gifts for the Cookie Jar

Muffins In A Jar

The Big Bake Sale Cookbook

Classic Tex-Mex and Texas Cooking

Classic Southwest Cooking

Miss Sadie's Southern Cooking

Texas Longhorn Cookbook

Cookbook 25 Years

A Little Taste of Texas

A Little Taste of Texas II

Trophy Hunters'
Wild Game Cookbook

Cooking with Beer

Recipe Keeper

Leaving Home Cookbook
and Survival Guide

Classic Pennsylvania Dutch Cooking

Simple Old-Fashioned Baking

Healthy Cooking with 4 Ingredients

Best-Loved Canadian Recipes

Best-Loved New England Recipes

Best-Loved Recipes from
the Pacific Northwest

Best-Loved Southern Recipes

The California Cookbook

The Pennsylvania Cookbook

www.cookbookresources.com
Your Ultimate Source for Easy Cookbooks

cookbook
resources ® LLC

www.cookbookresources.com